# CONTENTS

## Chapter One: Obesity

| | |
|---|---|
| Obesity | 1 |
| Childhood obesity at 'epidemic' levels | 4 |
| Parents to 'outlive obese youngsters' | 5 |
| Food industry blamed for surge in obesity | 6 |
| Obesity | 7 |
| Obesity and overweight | 10 |
| NHS wakes up to child obesity crisis | 11 |
| Tackling obesity in England | 12 |
| Obesity factfile | 12 |
| The deal with diets | 13 |
| 20 per cent of Britons will be clinically obese by 2017 | 14 |

## Chapter Two: Eating Disorders

| | |
|---|---|
| About eating disorders . . . | 15 |
| Causes of eating disorders | 17 |
| Fighting Anna | 18 |
| Risks | 20 |
| Men get eating disorders too | 21 |
| Common misconceptions | 22 |
| Women who go to extremes to lose weight | 24 |

| | |
|---|---|
| Thin is not the answer | 26 |
| I think my friend may have an eating disorder | 27 |
| Carers' questions | 28 |
| Eating disorders can be prevented! | 30 |

## Chapter Three: Body Image

| | |
|---|---|
| Body image | 31 |
| Body image | 32 |
| The fat of the land | 33 |
| Young girls who think they are too fat to be perfect | 34 |
| Don't put your daughter on a diet | 35 |
| You are not a model, you are a real person! | 36 |
| Body image and eating disorders | 37 |
| Image obsession | 38 |
| Ten steps to positive image | 39 |

| | |
|---|---|
| Key Facts | 40 |
| Additional Resources | 41 |
| Index | 42 |
| Acknowledgements | 44 |

# Introduction

*Obesity and Eating Disorders* is the seventy-second volume in the **Issues** series. The aim of this series is to offer up-to-date information about important issues in our world.

*Obesity and Eating Disorders* examines obesity, eating disorders and body image.

The information comes from a wide variety of sources and includes:
Government reports and statistics
Newspaper reports and features
Magazine articles and surveys
Web site material
Literature from lobby groups
and charitable organisations.

It is hoped that, as you read about the many aspects of the issues explored in this book, you will critically evaluate the information presented. It is important that you decide whether you are being presented with facts or opinions. Does the writer give a biased or an unbiased report? If an opinion is being expressed, do you agree with the writer?

*Obesity and Eating Disorders* offers a useful starting-point for those who need convenient access to information about the many issues involved. However, it is only a starting-point. At the back of the book is a list of organisations which you may want to contact for further information.

*****

# Obesity

## The new face of poverty for young women in Britain. Information from the YWCA

While anorexia, a condition resulting from chronic undereating, has received considerable public debate in recent years, obesity, caused by overeating and lack of physical exercise, has been virtually ignored. This is despite the fact that obesity poses equally serious health risks, in addition to psycho-social issues. Evidence from research suggests that:

- Over half of all women in Britain are either overweight or obese.
- One in three girls aged eleven are overweight.
- Among 16- to 24-year-olds, twice as many young women as young men are seriously obese.
- Obesity has a direct link with poverty and social exclusion.
- The risk of a heart attack for an obese woman is about three times that of a non-obese woman of the same age.
- The prevalence rates are particularly high among young women in low income groups and in the deprived minority ethnic groups in Britain such as Pakistanis and Black Caribbean.
- By the age of 15, only 36 per cent

of girls are engaged in physical activity for at least 30 minutes on most days compared to 71 per cent of boys.

## What is obesity?

Obesity is a condition in which a person's weight gain seriously endangers their health. It can result in serious medical problems. The four most common conditions are heart disease, type 2 diabetes (non-insulin dependent), high blood pressure and osteoarthritis. Obese women are twelve times more likely to develop type 2 diabetes than women of a healthy weight (Reaven 1995).

## The rise in obesity among women and girls

There has been a substantial rise in obesity amongst women and girls in the UK in the last twenty years, reflecting an increase in the developed countries as a whole. Levels for women have almost trebled from eight per cent in 1980 to 21 per cent in 1998.

Corresponding figures for men are lower at six and 17 per cent (Joint Health Surveys Unit 1999).

Over half of all women in Britain are either overweight or obese (National Audit Office 2001). Recent research suggests that not only are more adult women becoming overweight or obese, but rates have significantly increased in the younger age groups since the mid 1980s (Chinn and Rona 2001) and that one in three 11-year-old girls is now overweight (Rudolf 2001).

Among 16- to 24-year-olds, twice as many young women as young men are seriously obese (Joint Health Surveys Unit 1998).

The link between social class and obesity is also particularly strong for women. The prevalence of obesity was only 14 per cent in the highest social class (Social Class 1) whereas in the lowest (Social Class 5), double the number were obese (Joint Health Surveys Unit 1999). Higher than

average levels of obesity have been found amongst some minority ethnic groups. In the 16 to 34 age group, 19.5 per cent of Black Caribbean and 15 per cent of Pakistani young women are obese, compared with 12.7 per cent of women of the same age in the general population (Joint Health Surveys Unit 2001).

## Social factors causing obesity
### Poverty
Research evidence suggests that obesity has a direct link with poverty (Joint Health Surveys Unit 1999). The lower the income, the higher the tendency towards a fast-food diet with little nutritional value. Additionally, people with little disposable income are less motivated to engage in regular exercise due to the high costs associated with enrolling in a gym or sports club.

The rate of physical activity is even lower among some minority ethnic groups. Recent research indicates that one-third of Pakistani women aged 16-34 had not done any moderate or vigorous activity in the four weeks preceding the survey, compared to 16 per cent of young women and eight per cent of young men in the general population (Joint Health Surveys Unit 2001). The Pakistani community is one of poorest minority ethnic groups in the UK (Modood et al 1998). In addition, there are cultural issues. Group physical activity for women in the Pakistani and other Muslim communities is only encouraged if it is done in women-only settings. Such provision is woefully too few and far between.

### Unhealthy diet and lifestyle
Smoking is on the increase among young women. There are more young women smoking than young men. Twenty-six per cent of 15-year-old girls are now regular smokers (National Centre for Social Research and National Foundation for Educational Research 2001). Smoking is now cited by young women as a reason for giving up physical activity. Smokers felt they would be shown up as unfit; that the benefits of exercising would be cancelled out by smoking and that there was less need for physical activity as a means of

weight control because they used smoking to regulate their weight instead.

Alcohol consumption amongst young women is also on the increase with 46 per cent of 15-year-old girls drinking an average of 11.2 units a week (NCSR & NFER op cit). Alcohol consumption, coupled with an unhealthy diet of fast food, were seen as barriers to taking part in physical activity for fear of appearing unfit and because they cancelled out the positive benefits of exercise.

A high fat diet, especially the consumption of saturated fats, has been linked to obesity. Fatty foods are high in calories and tend not to satisfy the appetite so that overeating is more likely. The proportion of fat in the UK diet has increased dramatically since the Second World War from around 20 per cent to 40 per cent of total energy consumed (Association for the Study of Obesity 1997).

A recent survey of the diet and nutrition of young people aged 4-18 found that their diets tend to be high in saturated fats, sugar and salt. The most commonly eaten foods were white bread, savoury snacks, potato chips, biscuits, potatoes and chocolate. Girls were found to eat, by weight, more than four times as much sweets and chocolate than leafy green vegetables and to drink two-thirds more fizzy drinks than milk (Gregory 2000). Not only are girls and young women eating too much sugar, salt and saturated fats and not enough fruit and vegetables, but they are also more likely than young men to have erratic eating habits linked to concerns about their weight.

### Pressure to look like supermodels
A study found almost half of young women aged 16-24 were trying to lose weight and even amongst those with a desirable weight, 45 per cent were 'dieting' to lose it (Joint Health Studies Unit 1998).

The social pressure on women to look like supermodels has meant that girls as young as five are becoming weight conscious and consequently vulnerable to chronic

binge eating in later life. Rather than controlling their weight, excessive dieting often has the opposite effect. Periods of abstention are generally followed by binges and overeating resulting in weight gain.

Research has shown that mothers' attitudes to food influence their daughters' eating habits and weight outcomes. Mothers who experience compulsive eating habits are likely to pass on these habits to their daughters (Cutting 1999).

### Anxiety about safety
There is a heightened anxiety today about child abduction which has resulted in parents discouraging girls, in particular, to play out in public areas or to walk to the shops and to school on their own (Furedi 2001). Boys are considered to be less at risk – they are nearly twice as likely as girls to play in team games out of school (Rowe and Champion 2000).

Between 1986 and 1996, the proportion of under 17-year-olds walking to school fell from 59 to 49 per cent, whilst the number of car journeys to school has nearly doubled (DETR 1999). For girls and young women, opportunities for physical activity outside the home have diminished significantly with the rise in concern for their safety.

### Opting out of school sports
For girls, the level of participation in school sports and PE has dropped significantly over the years. Recent research indicated that 40 per cent of girls drop out of sports and PE by the age of 13 (Kirk 2000). Girls' participation in keep fit/aerobics – a form of exercise though to be favoured by girls – has regrettably dropped from 24 per cent in 1994 to

17 per cent in 1999, as has participation in extra-curricular netball (Rowe and Champion 2000). Although the rates of physical activity decrease for both sexes as children grow up, the decline is particularly marked amongst young women. A detailed survey of the health of young people between 1995 and 1997 found that by the age of 15, only 36 per cent of girls engaged in physical activity for at least 230 minutes on most days, compared to 71 per cent of boys (Joint Health Surveys Unit 1998).

A study of young women's attitudes to physical activity found that a key barrier to girls and young women's participation in school sports and physical activity in general was the requirement to wear old-fashioned PE kits and the use of communal showers (Kirk 2000). Teenage girls are far more self-conscious about their body image than females in any other age group. Having to parade in front of male peers wearing gym slips and to shower communally, therefore, is not conducive to their enjoyment of PE and sports and consequently acts as a disincentive.

Sports facilities outside school are often no better. Young women often find sports centres, clubs and gyms intimidating, alien and expensive. The range of activities on offer may be unappealing to their age group and there are few opportunities to participate in fun activities such as netball, roller skating and dance. Popular team sports such as football and cricket which are linked to a social scene are still male dominated and there are no equivalents for young women. In 1999, 32 per cent of boys were members of a football club compared with three per cent of girls (Rowe and Champion 2000).

## Psycho-social effects of obesity

In addition to the various medical conditions linked to obesity, there are psycho-social effects, to which women are more vulnerable than men. Low self-esteem has been identified in research as the most serious and enduring of all. Young women who are obese are more likely to suffer from low self-esteem and feelings of rejection and shame than young men (Hill and Williams 1998; Brown et al 2000). In a study of schoolgirls, obesity was considered to be a social stigma and obese girls were perceived by their peers to be passive, unattractive, unhealthy, weak-willed and having inferior physical abilities and poor self-control in dietary habits (McIntyre 1998).

### Sources:

Association for the Study of Obesity (1997) *Why do people become obese?* factsheet.

Brown W et al (2000) Relationship between body mass index and well-being in young Australian women. In *Int J Obesity* 24: 1360-1368.

Chinn S, Rona RJ (2001) Prevalence and trends in overweight and obesity in three cross sectional studies of British children, 1974-94. In *British Medical Journal* 322, 24-26.

Cutting T et al (1999) Like mother, like daughter: familial patterns of overweight are mediated by mothers' dietary disinhibition. In *American Journal of Clinical Nutrition*, Vol 69, No. 4, 608-613.

DETR (1999) *Transport Statistics Bulletin*, National Travel Survey 1996-1998 Update.

Furedi F (2001) *Paranoid Parenting, Abandon Your Anxieties and be a Good Parent.* Allen Lane, The Penguin Press.

Gregory J, et al (2000) *National Diet and Nutrition Survey: Young People Aged 14-18 Years.* Volume 1: Report of the Diet and Nutrition Survey. The Stationery Office.

Hill A and Williams J (1998) Psychological health in a non-clinical sample of obese women. In *Int J Obesity* 22: 578-583.

Joint Surveys Unit on behalf of the Department of Health (2001): *Health Survey for England: The Health of Minority Ethnic Groups '99.* The Stationery Office.

Joint Surveys Unit on behalf of the Department of Health (1999): *Health Survey for England: Cardiovascular Disease '98.* The Stationery Office.

Joint Health Surveys Unit on behalf of the Department of Health (1998) *Health Survey for England: The Health of Young People '95-'97.* The Stationery Office.

Kirk D (2000) *Towards Girl Friendly Physical Education.* Youth Sports Trust.

McIntyre AM (1998). Burden of Illness Review of Obesity: Are the true costs realised? In *J Roy Soc Health*, Vol. 118, No.2.

Modood et al (1997) *Ethnic Minorities in Britain.* Police Studies Institute.

National Audit Office (2001). *Tackling Obesity in England.* The Stationery Office.

National Centre for Social Research and National Foundation for Educational Research (2001) *Survey of Smoking, Drinking and Drug Use among Young Teenagers in 2000, 2001, 2002.* Interim findings.

Reaven G (1995): Are Insulin Resistance and/or Compensatory Hyperinsulinaemia involved in the Aetiology and Clinical Course of Patients with Hypertension? In *Int J Obesity* 19, Suppl 1, S2-S5.

Rowe N, Champion R (2000) *Young People and Sport, National Survey 1999.* Sport England.

Rudolf M et al (2001) Increasing prevalence of obesity in primary school children: cohort study. In *British Medical Journal* 322, 1094-1095.

■ The YWCA is a leading women's organisation and one of the oldest in the UK. Through their network of youth and community projects in England and Wales, they provide services to women to enable them to meet their full potential as individuals. The above information is an extract from one of their briefings. For more information on YWCA or their briefings, please contact the Policy and Campaigns Department on 01865 304215 or e-mail campaigns@ywca-gb.org.uk alternatively visit their web site at www.ywca-gb.org.uk

# Childhood obesity at 'epidemic' levels

Childhood obesity in Britain has reached epidemic levels and is likely to become even more common as children become less active, a leading health expert warned today.

Dr John Reilly, from the University of Glasgow, told a conference in Bristol that the growing number of obese children was likely to have serious implication for the general health and psychological welfare of the population.

At a joint conference of the Association of the Study of Obesity and the University of Bristol, Dr Reilly said obese children were now much more likely to remain overweight as they went through adulthood than they were 20 years ago.

He warned that they were at an increased risk of developing heart disease, diabetes or problems with their joints and bones in later life.

'It is a fairly common perception among families and health professionals that it [childhood obesity] does not matter that much,' he said.

'But childhood obesity does matter. It has adverse health implications both in the short term and the long term.

'We will get a lot more long-standing obesity than we have ever had previously – and that is a lot more dangerous.'

After his presentation, Dr Reilly said childhood obesity was a problem that had been around for two decades but which had only been widely recognised in the last few years.

'The epidemic started in the mid-1980s and as far as we can tell it is becoming more and more common,' he said.

'We have seen very dramatic increases right through the 1990s, and all the signs suggest it is going to get worse before it gets better.'

Dr Reilly said obesity among the young was becoming more common because children were leading much less active lifestyles – watching more television and playing video games – while being taken to school by car rather than walking.

'Both parents and children are much less active than they were,' he said. 'The environment now promotes obesity in a way that it did not do before.'

Dr Reilly said obesity in the young had short-term health implications, such as hypertension, high cholesterol and respiratory problems.

But he warned that these were unlikely to seriously affect children until they became much older, describing obesity as a 'silent problem', the effects of which only became apparent during adulthood.

He said childhood obesity was also linked to a number of mental health problems such as low self-esteem, caused by the teasing and bullying overweight children were often forced to endure.

'Obese children are subject to a lot of psychological pressure,' he said.

Dr Reilly also warned that obese children have poorer social, educational and economic prospects in adulthood than thinner young people. 'Adults who were obese as children also have poorer social, educational and economic prospects,' he said.

> **The growing number of obese children is likely to have serious implication for the general health and psychological welfare of the population**

'Childhood obesity has a high cost in health and economic terms and we should be making greater efforts to prevent it.'

Tomorrow the conference is due to hear the findings of a long-term study of children's diets.

Dr Pauline Emmett, one of the researchers on the Avon longitudinal study of parents and children, said: 'We found that children's diets are influenced by the educational level of their mother and that groups with the least educated mothers had higher levels of obesity.

'Our findings show that it is important that health professionals have a role especially in encouraging the less educated mothers to follow best practice.'

© Guardian Newspapers Limited 2003

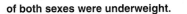

## Overweight or obese young adults

The graph below shows the proportion of young adults surveyed who were overweight or obese. Of young men and women aged 16-24, 6% and 8% respectively were obese, and a further 23% and 19% respectively were overweight. 17% of both sexes were underweight.

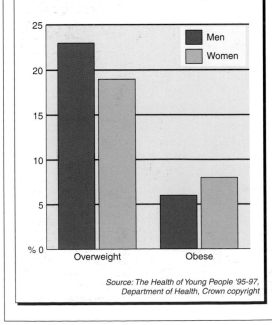

Source: The Health of Young People '95-97, Department of Health, Crown copyright

# Parents to 'outlive obese youngsters'

*By Roger Highfield*

Today's generation of children could die before their parents because of the soaring rates of obesity, the British Association for the Advancement of Science was told yesterday.

In the United States, where more than half of some groups – middle American white women, and black and Hispanic women – are clinically obese, there are already cases of this happening.

> ## The younger a person becomes obese, the worse the consequences for future health, from stroke to high blood pressure

Adolescents are becoming 'massively obese' at a very young age in America, a trend that is being mirrored in Britain, where more than one-fifth of the population is now clinically obese, Prof Andrew Prentice of the London School of Hygiene and Tropical Medicine told the association's meeting in Leicester.

But the prospects for parents will worsen, too, because of the combination of high-energy diet and dwindling exercise. If current trends continue, Prof Prentice said, in three generations' time, 'we will all be fat and all face the same health risk'.

Britain has abandoned targets to tackle obesity because of the lack of success in addressing the problem, but multinationals, notably fast food companies, could also do more to help. 'We need action in every walk of life,' he said.

The 30,000 people who die each year for obesity-related reasons in Britain have had nine years cut off their lifespan and the number and reduction in lifespan are likely to increase.

The younger a person becomes obese, the worse the consequences for future health, from stroke to high blood pressure, he said. 'The longer you are obese, the more likely you are to accrue all the damaging side-effects.'

Adult diseases such as angina and heart attacks are beginning to be seen in children. And type two diabetes – once called adult-onset diabetes – is now 'alarmingly common' in teenagers.

'When you put all these pieces together then you do come to the prediction that young people, who are being ambushed by this change in the environment, are storing up for themselves enormous ill health for the future,' Prof Prentice said.

'We are in an absolutely fascinating period in human evolution,' he said. Changes in diet had led to a height spurt over the past two centuries. 'Now we are going outwards in terms of girth,' he said.

In the mid-term, obesity drugs would be developed that would in turn have a major impact on health budgets, he said.

> ## Adult diseases such as angina and heart attacks are beginning to be seen in children. And type two diabetes is now 'alarmingly common' in teenagers

'My problem is that they are trying to find a cure for normal physiology.

'Obesity is not a disease – it is a normal biological response to the way we now live. And the drug companies are in this rather strange dilemma, if you like, of actually trying to find a cure for something that is not broken in the first place.'

# Food industry blamed for surge in obesity

*By Sarah Boseley,*
*Health Editor*

At least three in four of British men and women will be overweight within 10 to 15 years, according to health professionals who accuse governments of failing to tackle the problem because of fear of the food and drink industry.

An extraordinary rise in the numbers of the overweight and obese has taken place in the last 20 years. In 1980 6% of men and 8% of women were overweight. By the mid 1980s, that had doubled. Now 65.5% of men and 55.2% of women are overweight or obese in the UK, and the numbers are climbing.

A European Union summit on obesity in Copenhagen yesterday brought together government ministers and health professionals. They heard that obesity was becoming more of a threat than smoking.

A report from the International Obesity Taskforce said that a ban on tobacco advertising should be followed by restrictions to stop industry targeting children with adverts for junk food and sweets and prevent the installation of vending machines for soft drinks in schools.

'Officials are pretty terrified around the whole of Europe about how to confront some of these huge vested interests,' Philip James, chairman of the taskforce, told the summit.

'The fast food and soft drink industries have enormous vested interests which we need to confront.

> ## Tobacco advertising should be followed by restrictions to stop industry targeting children with adverts for junk food and sweets

If we don't, the epidemic of childhood obesity is going to rip through Europe so fast – with Britain being in the worst category – that we will have clinics of diabetic children of 13, where the evidence is clear that they will have major problems of blindness by the time they get into their 30s.

'Kidney units should be regearing because they are going to need huge numbers of kidney transplants and dialysis.'

Neville Rigby, director of public affairs at the taskforce, said there had been 'a quantum shift' in what was happening to people's body mass because of the changes in diet and lifestyle.

Between 1993 and 2000, the numbers of young men aged 16 to 24 classified as obese – with a body mass index of more than 30 – jumped from 4.9% to 9.3%. The rise in the 25 to 34 age group in the same seven years was from 10% to 20.3%. 'These should be the fit young men who are the pride of the nation,' he said.

Among 16- to 24-year-old women the rise was 11.1% to 15.7%. Even more alarming, he said, was a new category of super-obese women, with a body mass index of 40 or more. These women – so large they cannot tie their shoelaces or occupy a single seat on a bus – were 1% of the age group in 1993. By 2000 they were 2.4%.

Men and women who carry excess weight risk heart disease, cancers and diabetes. Type two diabetes, usually caused by obesity, used to be unknown in childhood but now paediatricians are having to learn how to treat it.

The couch-potato lifestyle had made weight problems worse, but the chief reason for the epidemic was diet, said the taskforce report, which criticises the industry for targeting children.

'Large business interests are involved in both promoting sedentary behaviour and the passive over-consumption of food,' it said. 'The food and drink industry seeks to focus on inactivity and promote sports to divert attention from the role of food and drinks. Analysis of marketing strategies shows a targeting of the young and particularly of pre-school children to establish brand preferences.'

© *Guardian Newspapers Limited 2003*

# Obesity

## Backgrounder on obesity and overweight

### Introduction

One of the most common problems related to lifestyle today is being overweight. Severe overweight or obesity is a key risk factor in the development of many chronic diseases such as heart and respiratory diseases, non-insulin-dependent diabetes mellitus or Type 2 diabetes, hypertension and some cancers, as well as early death. New scientific studies and data from life insurance companies have shown that the health risks of excessive body fat are associated with relatively small increases in bodyweight, not just with marked obesity.

Obesity and overweight are serious problems that pose a huge and growing financial burden on national resources. Fortunately, the conditions are largely preventable through sensible lifestyle changes.

### What is obesity and overweight?

Obesity is often defined simply as a condition of abnormal or excessive fat accumulation in the fat tissues (adipose tissue) of the body leading to health hazards. The underlying cause is a positive energy balance leading to weight gain i.e. when the calories consumed exceed the calories expended through activity.

In order to help people determine what their healthy weight is, a simple measure of the relationship between weight and height called the Body Mass Index (BMI) is used. BMI provides a useful tool that is commonly used by doctors and other health professionals to classify the prevalence of underweight, overweight and obesity in adults. It is defined as the weight in kilograms divided by the square of the height in metres ($kg/m^2$). For example, an adult who weighs 70 kg and whose height is 1.75 m will have a BMI of 22.9.

Overweight and obesity are classified as BMI in excess of 25 and 30, respectively. Typically, a BMI of

18.5 to 25 is considered 'healthy', a BMI of 25-29 is considered 'at risk' and a BMI of 30 or more is considered at 'high risk'.

### Body Mass Index
<18.5 Underweight
18.5 – 25 Healthy weight
25 – 30 Overweight
> 30 Obese

### Fat distribution: apples and pears

BMI still does not give us information about how fat is distributed in our body, which is important as abdominal excess of fat can have consequences in terms of health problems.

A way to measure fat distribution is the circumference of the waist. Waist circumference is unrelated to height and provides a simple and practical method of identifying overweight people who are at increased risk of obesity-related conditions. If waist circumference is greater than 94-102 cm for men and 80-88 cm for women, it means they have excess abdominal fat, which puts them at greater risk of health problems, even if their BMI is about right.

The waist circumference measurement divides people in two categories: individuals with an android fat distribution (often called 'apple' shape), meaning that most of their body fat is intra-abdominal and distributed around their stomach and chest and makes them at a greater risk of developing obesity-related diseases; and individuals with a gynoid fat distribution (often called 'pear' shape), meaning that most of their body fat is distributed around their hips, thighs and bottom. Obese men are more likely to be 'apples' while women are more likely to be 'pears'.

### The dynamics of energy balance: the bottom line?

The fundamental principle of energy balance is:

Changes in energy (fat) stores
=
energy (calorie) intake –
energy expenditure

Overweight and obesity are influenced by many factors including hereditary tendencies, environmental and behavioural factors, ageing and pregnancies. What is clear is that obesity is not always simply a result of overindulgence in highly palatable foods or of a lack of physical activity. Biological factors (hormones, genetics), stress, drugs and ageing also play a role.

However, dietary factors and physical activity patterns strongly influence the energy balance equation and they are also the major modifiable factors. Indeed, high-fat, energy-dense diets and sedentary lifestyles are the two characteristics most strongly associated with the increased prevalence of obesity worldwide. Conversely, weight loss occurs when energy intake is less

than energy expenditure over an extended period of time. A restricted calorie diet combined with increased physical activity is generally the advice proffered by dietitians for sustained weight loss.

Miracle or wonder diets that severely limit calories or restrict food groups should be avoided as they are often limiting in important nutrients and/or cannot be sustained for prolonged periods. Besides, they do not teach correct eating habits and can result in yo-yo dieting (the gain and loss of weight in cycles resulting from dieting followed by over-eating). This so-called yo-yo dieting may be dangerous to long-term health and can result in the loss of lean body mass. This in turn lowers the metabolism making it successively even harder to lose weight.

## What are the trends in obesity and overweight?

Evidence is now emerging to suggest that the prevalence of overweight and obesity is rising dramatically worldwide and that the problem appears to be increasing rapidly in children as well as in adults.

The most comprehensive data on the prevalence of obesity world-wide are those of the World Health Organisation (WHO) MONICA project (MONItoring of trends and determinants in CArdiovascular diseases study). Together with information from national surveys, the data show that the prevalence of obesity in most European countries has increased by about 10-40% in the past 10 years, ranging from 10-20% in men and 10-25% in women. The most alarming increase has been observed in the UK, where nearly two-thirds of men and over half of women are overweight or obese.

## What are the health consequences of obesity and overweight?

The health consequences of obesity and overweight are many and varied, ranging from an increased risk of premature death to several non-fatal but debilitating and psychological complaints that can have an adverse effect on quality of life.

The major adverse health problems associated with obesity and overweight are:

- Type 2 diabetes
- Cardiovascular diseases and hypertension
- Respiratory diseases (sleep apnea syndrome)
- Some cancers
- Osteoarthritis
- Psychological problems
- Alteration of the quality of life

The degree of risk is influenced by the relative amount of excess bodyweight, the location of the body fat, the extent of weight gain during adulthood and amount of physical activity. Most of these problems can be improved with relatively modest weight loss (10 to 15%), especially if physical activity is increased too.

### Type 2 diabetes

Of all serious diseases, it is Type 2 diabetes (the type of diabetes which normally develops in adulthood) or non-insulin-dependent diabetes mellitus (NIDDM), which has the strongest association with obesity and overweight. Indeed, the risk of developing Type 2 diabetes rises with a BMI that is well below the cut-off point for obesity (BMI of 30). Women who are obese are 12 times more likely to develop Type 2 diabetes than women of healthy weight. The risk of Type 2 diabetes increases with BMI, especially in those with a family history of diabetes, and decreases with weight loss.

### Cardiovascular disease and hypertension

Cardiovascular disease (CVD) includes coronary heart disease (CHD), stroke and peripheral vascular disease. These diseases account for a large proportion (up to one-third) of deaths in men and women in most industrialised countries and their incidence is increasing in developing countries.

Obesity predisposes an individual to a number of cardio-vascular risk factors, including hypertension and raised blood cholesterol. In women, obesity is the third most powerful predictor of CVD after age and blood pressure. The risk of heart attack for an obese woman is about three times that of a lean woman of the same age.

Obese individuals are more likely to have raised blood tri-glycerides (blood fats), low density lipoprotein (LDL) cholesterol ('bad cholesterol') and decreased high density lipoprotein (HDL) cholesterol ('good cholesterol'). This metabolic profile is most often seen

## Risk of associated diseases of obesity

The table below indicates the extent to which obesity increases the risks of developing a number of these diseases relative to the non-obese population. The relative risks are based on a comprehensive review of international literature.

| Disease | Relative risk – women | Relative risk – men |
|---|---|---|
| Type 2 diabetes* | 12.7 | 5.2 |
| Hypertension | 4.2 | 2.6 |
| Myocardial Infarction | 3.2 | 1.5 |
| Cancer of the Colon | 2.7 | 3.0 |
| Angina | 1.8 | 1.8 |
| Gall Bladder Diseases | 1.8 | 1.8 |
| Ovarian Cancer | 1.7 | – |
| Osteoarthritis | 1.4 | 1.9 |
| Stroke | 1.3 | 1.3 |

*Non-insulin dependent diabetes mellitus (NIDDM)

Note: The BMI range for the obese and non-obese groups used to estimate relative risk varies between studies, which limits the comparability of these data.

Source: National Audit Office estimates based on literature review (Appendix 6)

in obese people with a high accumulation of intra-abdominal fat ('apples') and has consistently been related to an increased risk of CHD. With weight loss, the levels of blood lipids (fats) can be expected to return to normal. For every 1 kg of weight lost, LDL cholesterol has been estimated to decrease by 1%. A 10 kg weight loss can produce a 15% decrease in LDL cholesterol levels and an 8% increase in HDL cholesterol.

*The health consequences of obesity and overweight are many and varied, ranging from an increased risk of premature death to several non-fatal but debilitating and psychological complaints*

The association between hypertension (high blood pressure) and obesity is well documented and the proportion of hypertension attributable to obesity has been estimated to be 30-65% in Western populations. In fact, blood pressure increases with BMI; for every 10 kg increase in weight, blood pressure rises by 2-3mm Hg. Conversely, weight loss induces a fall in blood pressure and typically, for each 1% reduction in bodyweight, blood pressure falls by 1-2mm Hg.

The prevalence of hypertension in overweight individuals is nearly three times higher than that for non-overweight adults and the risk in overweight individuals aged 20-44 years of hypertension is nearly six times greater than that for non-overweight adults.

## Cancer

Although the link between obesity and cancer is less well defined, several studies have found an association between overweight and the incidence of certain cancers, particularly of hormone-dependent and gastrointestinal cancers. Greater risks of breast, endometrial, ovarian and cervical cancers have been documented for obese women, and there is some evidence of increased risk of prostate and rectal cancer in men. The clearest association is with cancer of the colon, for which obesity increases the risk by nearly three times in both men and women.

## Osteoarthritis

Degenerative diseases of the weight-bearing joints, such as the knee, are very common complications of obesity and overweight. Mechanical damage to joints resulting from excess weight is generally thought to be the cause. Pain in the lower back is also more common in obese people and may be one of the major contributors to obesity-related absences from work.

## Psychological aspects

Obesity is highly stigmatised in many European countries in terms both of perceived undesirable bodily appearance and of the character defects that it is supposed to indicate. Even children as young as six perceive obese children as 'lazy, dirty, stupid, ugly, liars and cheats'.

Obese people have to contend with discrimination. Studies show that overweight young women in the UK and USA earn significantly less than healthy women who are not overweight or than women with other chronic health problems.

Compulsive overeating also occurs with increased frequency among obese people and many people with this eating disorder have a long history of bingeing and weight fluctuations.

## What is the economic cost of obesity and overweight?

International studies on the economic costs of obesity have shown that they account for between 2% and 7% of total health care costs, the level depending on the way the analysis is undertaken. In France, for example, the direct cost of obesity-related diseases (including the costs of personal health care, hospital care, physician services and drugs for diseases with a well-established relationship with obesity) amounted to about 2% of total health care expenditure. In the Netherlands, the proportion of the country's total general practitioner expenditure attributable to obesity and overweight is around 3-4%.

In England, the estimated annual financial cost of obesity is £0.5 billion in treatment costs to the National Health Service and the impact on the economy is estimated to be around £2 billion. The estimated human cost of obesity is 18 million sick days a year; 30,000 deaths a year, resulting in 40,000 lost years of working life and a shortened lifespan of nine years on average.

## What groups are responsible for promoting healthy lifestyles?

Promoting healthy diets and increased levels of physical activity to control overweight and obesity must involve the active participation of many groups including governments, health professionals, the food industry, the media and consumers. Their shared responsibility is to help promote healthy diets that are low in fat, high in complex carbohydrates and which contain large amounts of fresh fruits and vegetables.

Greater emphasis on improved opportunities for physical activity is clearly needed, especially with increased urbanisation, the ageing of the population and the parallel increase in time devoted to sedentary pursuits.

# Obesity and overweight

## Information from the World Health Organization (WHO)

Obesity has reached epidemic proportions globally, with more than 1 billion adults overweight – at least 300 million of them clinically obese – and is a major contributor to the global burden of chronic disease and disability. Often coexisting in developing countries with undernutrition, obesity is a complex condition, with serious social and psychological dimensions, affecting virtually all ages and socioeconomic groups.

Increased consumption of more energy-dense, nutrient-poor foods with high levels of sugar and saturated fats, combined with reduced physical activity, have led to obesity rates that have risen threefold or more since 1980 in some areas of North America, the United Kingdom, Eastern Europe, the Middle East, the Pacific Islands, Australasia and China. The obesity epidemic is not restricted to industrialised societies; this increase is often faster in developing countries than in the developed world.

Obesity and overweight pose a major risk for serious diet-related chronic diseases, including type 2 diabetes, cardiovascular disease, hypertension and stroke, and certain forms of cancer. The health consequences range from increased risk of premature death, to serious chronic conditions that reduce the overall quality of life. Of especial concern is the increasing incidence of child obesity.

### Facts:

■ Globally, there are more than 1 billion overweight adults, at least 300 million of them obese.

■ Obesity and overweight pose a major risk for chronic diseases, including type 2 diabetes, cardiovascular disease, hypertension and stroke, and certain forms of cancer.

■ The key causes are increased consumption of energy-dense foods high in saturated fats and sugars, and reduced physical activity.

### Why is this happening?

The rising epidemic reflects the profound changes in society and in behavioural patterns of communities over recent decades. While genes are important in determining a person's susceptibility to weight gain, energy balance is determined by calorie intake and physical activity. Thus societal changes and worldwide nutrition transition are driving the obesity epidemic. Economic growth, modernisation, urbanisation and globalisation of food markets are just some of the forces thought to underlie the epidemic.

As incomes rise and populations become more urban, diets high in complex carbohydrates give way to more varied diets with a higher proportion of fats, saturated fats and sugars. At the same time, large shifts towards less physically demanding work have been observed worldwide. Moves towards less physical activity are also found in the increasing use of automated transport, technology in the home, and more passive leisure pursuits.

### How do we define obesity and overweight?

The prevalence of overweight and obesity is commonly assessed by using body mass index (BMI), defined as the weight in kilograms divided by the square of the height in metres ($kg/m^2$). A BMI over 25 $kg/m^2$ is defined as overweight, and a BMI of over 30 $kg/m^2$ as obese. These markers provide common benchmarks for assessment, but the risks of disease in all populations can increase progressively from lower BMI levels.

Adult mean BMI levels of 22-23 $kg/m^2$ are found in Africa and Asia, while levels of 25-27 $kg/m^2$ are prevalent across North America, Europe, and in some Latin American, North African and Pacific Island countries. BMI increases amongst middle-aged elderly people, who are at the greatest risk of health complications. In countries undergoing nutrition transition, overnutrition often coexists with undernutrition. People with a BMI below 18.5 $kg/m^2$ tend to be underweight.

*Obesity is a complex condition, with serious social and psychological dimensions, affecting virtually all ages and socioeconomic groups*

The distribution of BMI is shifting upwards in many populations. And recent studies have shown that people who were undernourished in early life and then become obese in adulthood, tend to develop conditions such as high blood pressure, heart disease and diabetes at an earlier age and in more severe form than those who were never undernourished.

■ The above information is from *Obesity and Overweight*. Geneva, World Health Organization, 2003. Available on the Internet at http://www.who.int/hpr/NPH/docs/gs_obesity.pdf (WHO material in the Issues project book does not imply any endorsement of the book by WHO).

# NHS wakes up to child obesity crisis

**Clinic to help overweight children could be first of many. By Jo Revill**

The growing epidemic of child obesity has prompted the National Health Service to open its first clinic to deal with the problem.

Following revelations last week that an 11-year-old girl weighed 20 stone, doctors yesterday called for parents to be given much more detailed instructions on how to manage the diet and exercise patterns of their children.

Obesity in the young is now seen as a soaring health crisis, with one in five of all nine-year-olds estimated to be overweight, and one in 10 obese – a rate that has doubled in the last two decades.

For some unhappy children, the cure can be drastic. Leeds schoolgirl Gemma Taylor revealed last week how she may need a stomach-stapling operation to curb her food intake. She weighs 20 stone and has to buy size 30 clothes. Her parents, who are also overweight, are worried that she could be badly bullied at school, and that she faces life-threatening problems if she cannot have the necessary surgery.

If the doctors decide she is too young for the surgery, Gemma might find help at the clinics being planned by Dr Mary Rudolf, the paediatrician who has helped the initiative with the East Leeds Primary Care Trust.

'We have to start tackling this in childhood before lifestyle habits are set for ever,' said Rudolf, who last year published research showing high rates of morbidly obese children in her district. 'Our approach is to make people aware of what they are eating, and their level of physical activity or lack of it. We may use diaries so that they can keep a record of their habits, but we need to give them practical suggestions of what they can do. It's no use making them worried if we can't offer achievable solutions.'

Her clinic will start in January and, uniquely, will not be staffed by health professionals but by workers trained to talk to families. It will involve working with school nurses, doctors, the local leisure centre and dietitians to provide a week-by-week course of action for around 70 children a year.

If this pilot scheme is shown to be a success, it could be replicated around Britain. But reversing the long-term trend is going to be one of the biggest challenges facing society.

Rudolf said: 'This problem stretches right across Britain. It's down to a lack of physical activity as children no longer play outside but watch TV or play on computer games instead.'

---

### Obesity in the young is now seen as a soaring health crisis

---

No one should be in doubt about the potentially devastating consequences of childhood obesity. It has led to the first cases of Type 2 diabetes being seen in the UK among teenagers. In children, as in adults, carrying around many extra stones of weight causes hypertension (high blood pressure), an increased tendency of the blood to clot and a cluster of different cardiovascular problems. It is linked to difficulties in breathing during sleep, asthma and serious liver and kidney conditions.

Some research has been carried out on whether there is a genetic basis for obesity. So far five specific genetic mutations have been identified affecting children. But a predisposition to obesity appears largely to be caused by a complex interaction between as least 250 obesity-associated genes. Other factors, such as what food mothers eat during pregnancy, or a decision not to breastfeed, are now being studied for their relevance.

A more insidious factor is also being blamed for the rise in overweight children. American and British children are exposed to around 10 food commercials for every hour of television that they watch. Most of the commercials are bright and jazzy and sell fast food, soft drinks, sweets and sugar-sweetened breakfast cereal.

Because of concerns over the ads, the Food Standards Agency is to commission research which will look at the promotional activities carried out by the food industry and how they are linked to children's eating habits. This follows increasing disquiet both in Europe and in the United States about the aggressive marketing tactics used to sell junk food. In the United States, doctors recently singled out the promotion of Spiderman cereal, McDonald's Happy Meals and Pepsi Cola campaigns for exploiting children's desires.

The language being used against the food industry is getting stronger. Michael Brody, chair of the American Academy of Child and Adolescent Psychiatry's media committee, said recently: 'Just like paedophiles, marketers have become child experts.'

Yet there are few signs that the British Government wants to take any restrictive action, such as banning TV adverts in children's TV time, or curbing promotion of sugar-filled food. The only positive measure has been a plan to provide each child aged four to six with a free piece of fruit at school by 2004.

A spokeswoman for the Department of Health said: 'Nothing is being ruled in or out in future efforts to tackle obesity, but we are not currently considering restrictions on food advertising for children.'

■ This article first appeared in *The Observer*, 3 November 2002.

# Tackling obesity in England

Obesity occurs when a person puts on weight to the point that it seriously endangers health. Some people are more susceptible to weight gain for genetic reasons, but the fundamental cause of obesity is consuming more calories than are expended in daily life.

In 1980, eight per cent of women in England were classified as obese, compared to six per cent of men. By 1998, the prevalence of obesity had nearly trebled to 21 per cent of women and 17 per cent of men and there is no sign that the upward trend is moderating. Currently, over half of women and about two-thirds of men are either overweight or obese. The growth of obesity in England reflects a worldwide trend which is most marked in, though not restricted to, developed countries. Most evidence suggests that the main reason for the rising prevalence is a combination of less active lifestyles and changes in eating patterns.

Obesity has a substantial human cost by contributing to the onset of disease and premature mortality. It also has serious financial consequences for the National Health Service (NHS) and for the economy. Though there are inherent uncertainties in quantifying the link between obesity and associated disease, we estimate that it costs at least £$^1/_2$ billion a year in treatment costs to the NHS, and possibly in excess of £2 billion to the wider economy.

Obesity is not an easy problem to tackle, though even modest weight loss confers significant medical benefits. Against a background of rising prevalence, halting the upward trend presents a major challenge. Part of the solution lies in preventing people from becoming overweight and then obese, as much as helping those who are already obese. As a lifestyle issue, the scope for policy to effect such changes in a direct way is very limited. The Department of Health cannot by itself be expected to be able to 'cure' the problem.

## Key facts about obesity in England

The four most common problems linked to obesity:
- Heart disease
- Type 2 diabetes
- High blood pressure
- Osteoarthritis

- 1 in 5 adults is obese
- The number has trebled over the last 20 years

---

*The growth of obesity in England reflects a worldwide trend which is most marked in developed countries*

---

- Nearly two-thirds of men and over half of women are overweight or obese

*The estimated human cost:*
- 18 million sick days a year
- 30,000 deaths a year, resulting in 40,000 lost years of working life
- Deaths linked to obesity shorten life by 9 years on average

*The estimated financial cost:*
- £$^1/_2$ billion a year in treatment costs to the NHS
- Possibly £2 billion a year impact on the economy

■ The above information is from the executive summary of *Tackling obesity in England*, a document produced by the Comptroller and Auditor General.

© Crown copyright

## Obesity factfile

The incidence of obesity in England has trebled in the last 20 years.
- One in every five adults – around eight million in total – is obese
- Nearly two-thirds of men and more than half of women in England are now either overweight or obese
- Health problems linked to obesity are heart disease; Type 2, non-insulin dependent, diabetes; high blood pressure; osteoarthritis; and a number of cancers
- Deaths linked to obesity shorten life by nine years on average
- 30,000 deaths in 1998 were attributable to obesity
- Obesity was the cause of 18 million days of sickness absence in 1998 and 40,000 lost years of working life
- By 2010 obesity and its consequences are expected to cost the economy more than £3.6 billion a year.

### Definition of obesity

Obesity is most commonly defined in terms of body mass index (BMI). The BMI is calculated as follows:

Weight in kilograms / (height in metres squared) = BMI

A desirable BMI is considered to be in the region of 20 to 25. Above this is defined as 'overweight'. And a BMI over 30 is defined as 'obese'. Having a waist circumference of more than 37 inches (94 cm) if you are a man and 32 inches (80cm) if you are a woman means you could be increasing your risk of developing heart disease or diabetes.

■ The above information is from *NHS Magazine*'s web site which can be found at www.nhs.uk/nhsmagazine

© Crown copyright

# The deal with diets

## Information from KidsHealth.org

If you watch television, see movies, read newspapers, or flip through magazines, you've probably noticed that diets are everywhere. High-protein diets. Low-fat diets. All-vegetable diets. No-pasta diets. But with all the focus on dieting, how do you figure out what's healthy and what isn't?

Many teens feel pressured to lose weight and try different types of diets, but if you really need to lose weight, improving your eating habits and exercising will help you more than any diet. Keep reading to get the down-and-dirty basics on dieting.

### Why diet?

People diet for many reasons. Some teens are an unhealthy weight and need to pay closer attention to their eating and exercise habits. Some teens play sports and want to be in top physical condition. Other teens may feel they would look and feel better if they lost a few pounds.

Some teens may diet because they think they are supposed to look a certain way. Models and actresses are thin, and most fashions are represented and shown off by very thin models. But the model-thin style is based on an unrealistic look for most people. By around ages 12 or 13, most teen girls go through body changes that are natural and necessary: their hips broaden, their breasts develop, and suddenly the way they look may not match girls on TV or in magazine ads.

### Can diets be unhealthy?

Any diet on which you eat fewer calories than you need to get through the day without feeling like you're going to keel over – like an 800-calorie-per-day diet, for instance – is dangerous. Diets that don't allow any fat can also be bad for you. You should have a certain amount of fat in your diet, up to 30% of your total calories. Although a low-fat diet may be OK, don't go completely fat-free.

Don't fall for diets that restrict certain food groups, either. A diet that says no to breads or pastas or allows you to eat only fruit is unhealthy. You won't get the vitamins and minerals you need and although you may lose weight, you'll probably gain it back as soon as you start eating in your usual way.

Some teens start dieting because they think all the problems in their lives are because of weight. Or some teens have an area of their lives that they can't control – an alcoholic parent, for example – so they focus excessively on something they can control – their exercise and food. Once these teens start losing pounds, they may get lots of praise and compliments from friends and family that makes them feel good. But eventually they reach a weight plateau – they don't lose as much weight as before because their body is trying to maintain a healthy weight. They may also find they aren't any happier, but they still keep their main focus on their weight.

Some teens may find it hard to control their eating, so they control it for a little while, but then eat tons of food. Feeling guilty about the binge, they vomit or use laxatives. Eating too little to maintain a healthy weight (anorexia) or eating only to throw up the calories (bulimia) are both eating disorders, which are harmful to a person's health. A teen with an eating disorder needs medical treatment right away.

### So how can I lose weight safely?

The word diet usually means restricting calories or certain food groups. When you're a teen, dieting can be dangerous because you may not get the right kinds and amounts of nutrients, which can lead to poor growth and other health problems. In other words, by not eating right your height could even fall short!

But eating healthy meals and snacks combined with reasonable amounts of exercise may help you lose weight and develop properly at the same time. And guess what – for a lot of teens, just being more active might help you lose weight without even changing what you eat. Even if you don't lose weight, regular exercise will make you healthier and you will feel better about yourself. So get moving – whether you're involved in sports or you just take a walk or a bike ride several days a week, exercise really helps.

The most important diet do is to eat a wide variety of enough food to meet your body's needs. Try to cut back on high-fat meats (like burgers and hot dogs), eat more fruits and veggies, and drink more water instead of sugary drinks like sports drinks or sodas.

For many teens, just exercising more and eating healthily by using the Food Guide Pyramid can help you stay in shape and achieve a healthy weight. But if you are concerned about your body's size or think you need to lose weight, talk with your doctor or a registered dietitian.

A doctor or dietitian may reassure you that you are at a healthy weight. Or if you are overweight, he or she can sit down with you and determine the best way for you to reach a healthy weight.

## Great ways to find great health

If you want to change your health habits, here are some tried-and-true tips:

- Exercise!
- Drink milk, including fat-free or low-fat milk. (Many teens mistakenly think that milk has more calories than other drinks like soda. But a glass of skimmed milk has only 80 calories as well as protein and calcium. Soda has 120 calories of sugar and no other nutrients at all.)
- Eat a variety of foods, including plenty – at least five servings a day – of fruits and veggies. Remember that potato chips don't count!
- Drink plenty of water (at least four to six 8-ounce glasses a day).
- Eat lean, high-protein foods, like lean meat, chicken, fish, or beans.
- Eat grains, which provide fibre, B vitamins, and iron.
- Eat breakfast. Studies show that people who eat breakfast do better in school and tend to eat less throughout the day and are less likely to be overweight.
- Watch out for excessive caffeine – it doesn't help you lose weight and can cause dehydration. Many soft drinks contain caffeine, so check the label.
- Stay away from fad diets – even if you lose 5 pounds, you'll just gain it back when you go back to your usual way of eating.
- Don't take diet pills, even ones you get over the counter.
- Don't get into an 'I don't eat that' way of thinking, like 'I don't eat dairy foods.' If you eliminate entire food groups, you may miss out on important nutrients, like calcium.
- If you choose to become a vegetarian, talk to your doctor or dietitian about how to make nutritious vegetarian choices.

### Dieting danger signs

How do you know if your diet or a friend's diet is out of control? If you or a friend does any of the following things, talk to a trusted adult or doctor:

- continues to diet, even if not overweight

*Studies show that people who eat breakfast do better in school and tend to eat less throughout the day and are less likely to be overweight*

- has physical changes, such as weakness, headaches, or dizziness
- withdraws from family and friends
- performs poorly in school
- eats in secret
- thinks about food all the time
- restricts activities because of food or compulsive exercise
- fears food
- wears baggy clothes to hide thinness
- vomits after meals or uses laxatives

Dieting and weight control can consume your life. By accepting your body and making healthy choices, you'll keep your weight under control and enjoy life.

- This information was provided by KidsHealth, one of the largest resources online for medically reviewed health information written for parents, kids and teens. For more articles like this one, visit www.KidsHealth.org or else www.TeensHealth.org

© KidsHealth.org

---

# 20pc of Britons will be clinically obese by 2017

### By Sarah Womack, Social Affairs Correspondent

A fifth of Britain's population will be obese within the next 10 to 15 years, health experts said yesterday. They said Britons were on the way to becoming the fattest people in Europe, and catching up with the United States, which has the world's heaviest population.

The figures were disputed however by politicians who said the idea that one in five adults was heading towards 'superfat status' was absurd.

Most scientists measure obesity by calculating body mass – dividing a person's weight in kilograms by the square of their height in metres. An adult with a BMI of 30 or more is considered obese. Anyone with a score of 25 to 29.9 is overweight.

Critics say this means that a person is clinically obese when in fact they are just carrying a few extra pounds.

Gerry Steinberg, a Labour MP on the Commons Public Accounts Committee, criticised the 'ridiculous nanny state' politics which estimated that so many adults were dangerously fat. He said recently that if people ate and drank too much and took too little exercise, they had only themselves to blame.

But Prof Philip James, the chairman of the International Obesity Task Force, said it was that sort of attitude which was fuelling a public health disaster.

He estimated that 40 per cent of British people were overweight, while a further 20 per cent were approaching obesity, and said the European Union should ban advertisements for sugary drinks and junk food that target children.

Obesity and a lack of exercise is strongly linked with heart disease, stroke, diabetes and several types of cancer.

• Unhealthy people in Somerset are being advised to take up golf under a Taunton council scheme to help to improve fitness levels. The game is being included in its physical activity referral scheme under which family doctors prescribe exercise.

© Telegraph Group Limited, London 2003

# About eating disorders . . . ◆ ◆ ◆

**The person suffering from anorexia, bulimia and compulsive eating will be referred to as 'she'. However, most of what is said applies equally to the ten per cent or so of sufferers who are male**

### Anorexia nervosa

Anorexia is colloquially referred to as the 'slimmer's disease', but this title does not give a very useful description of the condition. Anorexia is a serious condition, and not merely an obsession with weight or slimming.

The medical label, anorexia nervosa, is also unhelpful for those trying to understand the condition. The term literally means 'loss of appetite from nervous origins' but the patient has usually conquered her appetite, not lost it. Although she may claim at the time to have no appetite, many recovered patients admit that they were often extremely hungry but refused themselves the right to eat.

A patient is diagnosed as suffering from anorexia nervosa when she fulfils the following criteria:

a. Refusal to maintain an adequate body weight
b. Intense fear of gaining weight or becoming fat, even though underweight
c. Cannot see how thin she is

d. In females, absence of at least three consecutive menstrual periods

### Bulimia nervosa

Bulimia means 'ox hunger' or voracious appetite. Other terms which have been used for the same syndrome include:

- the abnormal weight control syndrome
- the binge-purge syndrome
- the dietary chaos syndrome
- chaotic eating
- dysorexia and bulimarexia

The diagnostic criteria for bulimia nervosa are as follows:

a. Episodes of binge eating (rapidly eating a large amount of food) occurring at least twice a week for three months
b. A feeling of having no control over eating behaviour during the binges
c. Regularly engaging in either self-induced vomiting, use of laxatives or diuretics, strict dieting or fasting, or vigorous exercise, in order to prevent weight gain

d. Persistent over-concern with weight and shape.

### Relationship between anorexia and bulimia

There appears to be a lot of overlap between anorexia and bulimia. Some patients suffer from both conditions at the same time, and others swing from one to the other. The fear of being fat is central to both conditions, and both anorexics and bulimics may perceive themselves as being far fatter than they really are.

Although bulimics may be of normal weight or overweight while anorexics are by definition underweight, most bulimics and anorexics desire to be far below the ideal weight for their age and height. Some bulimics have lost as much weight as anorexics, but appear to be at a normal weight because they were overweight when they began to diet.

Depression is common among those suffering from either condition, and feelings of ineffectiveness, guilt, self-hatred and low self-esteem are virtually universal among sufferers.

Vomiting, laxative use and excessive exercise are used by both anorexics and bulimics to prevent weight gain. Most bulimics go through periods of extreme food restriction. A sub-group of anorexics occasionally give in to their bodily cravings and overeat, although this may not happen frequently enough for the patient to be labelled bulimic.

## Prevalence: How big a problem?

Anorexia and bulimia are not new conditions. Nevertheless, they appear to be becoming more and more prevalent among young females in Western society.

At least one in every two hundred adolescent girls in Britain is likely to suffer from anorexia nervosa. The figure given for female university students is one in fifty, while in departments of physical education and schools of dance or modelling, it is even higher, with one in every fourteen girls in these environments apparently suffering from anorexia nervosa.

The estimated prevalence of bulimia nervosa ranges from one per

cent to twenty per cent of all females, and from nought to five per cent of all males.

## Binge-eating disorder

The criteria for binge-eating are as follows:

a) Eating in a discrete period an amount of food that is definitely larger than most would eat during a similar period, couples with a sense of lack of control – a feeling that one cannot stop or control how much one eats

b) Episodes are associated with 3

or more of the following: excessively rapid eating; eating until uncomfortably full; eating large amounts when not hungry; eating alone because of embarrassment re eating; self-disgust, depression and/or guilt after overeating

c) Marked distress re binge eating

d) Occurs more than twice a week for 6 months

e) Not associated with regular use of inappropriate compensatory behaviours e.g. purging, fasting or excessive exercise.

## Compulsive overeating

Compulsive eating is an eating disorder which is similar to bulimia in many respects. Compulsive eaters may fulfil all of the diagnostic criteria listed above for bulimia nervosa except regular purging. Compulsive eaters either binge on large amounts of food or nibble snacks continuously throughout the day. This usually results in obesity, although some compulsive eaters remain at a normal weight as they also have 'binge-free' periods when they eat very little at all to keep their weight down.

Just because a woman eats large amounts and becomes obese does not mean that she is necessarily a compulsive eater. She may merely have a hearty appetite and enjoy her food.

A woman can be identified as a compulsive eater if she not only overeats but is obsessed with food, thinking about it continually. A compulsive eater feels emotionally 'empty' or unhappy. Her eating may be 'comfort eating', an attempt to soothe her hurts and relieve her depression. While she concentrates on food she can avoid underlying problems. She is likely to be upset about her overeating, and to criticise herself for it, feeling ashamed and guilty and hating herself for acting in this manner. Yet she feels unable to do anything about it, as she is unable to control herself when she feels the desire to eat.

■ The above information is from Anorexia and Bulimia Care's web site which can be found at www.anorexiabulimiacare.co.uk

© 2003 Anorexia and Bulimia Care

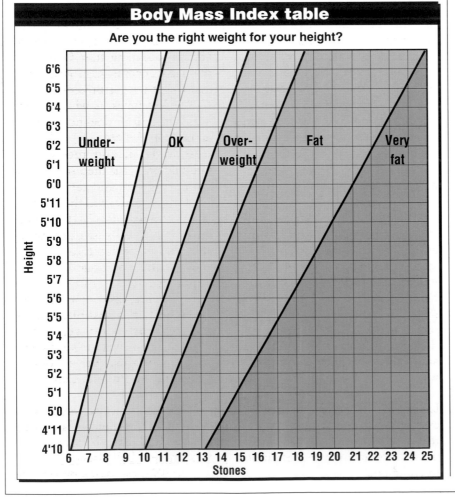

### Body Mass Index table
**Are you the right weight for your height?**

Height (feet/inches) vs Stones, with regions labelled: Underweight, OK, Overweight, Fat, Very fat.

Height axis: 4'10, 4'11, 5'0, 5'1, 5'2, 5'3, 5'4, 5'5, 5'6, 5'7, 5'8, 5'9, 5'10, 5'11, 6'0, 6'1, 6'2, 6'3, 6'4, 6'5, 6'6

Stones axis: 6, 7, 8, 9, 10, 11, 12, 13, 14, 15, 16, 17, 18, 19, 20, 21, 22, 23, 24, 25

# Causes of eating disorders

## Information from Anorexia and Bulimia Care

Many people are looking at the causes in connection with today's obsession with body image and the popular notion that 'thin is beautiful'. In addition we have health educationists informing us that we all overeat or eat too much fat and sugar.

There is no official data concerning the degree to which these factors are a cause and the medical world seems divided on the issue.

The most important aspect of eating disorders is low self-esteem, and some would say that this is caused by the fact that they are the wrong shape. In most cases this is not so. The poor self-image is due to much greater issues of emotional pain and feelings of rejection. When a person has enough stress to make her believe she is not 'up to the mark' she will try to find what the mark is. It is then that the media, modelling agencies and photographers give strong messages to young people who do not know what is wrong with them, or why they feel the way they do. Striving for the perfect body is the way that some take to make them feel better. However, once anorexia becomes entrenched the aim is, not to be perfect, but not to be – at all.

> *It is common for the parents of an anorexic to say she was a 'model child' who did what she was told and did not cause any bother*

It is not always helpful for the general public to be told we should eat less of anything because adolescents have no way of estimating what *less* means. In other words we are often not told what is acceptable – only what *isn't*.

Those people with a predisposition to eating disorders will react strongly to any suggestion that their body is not right for the job. Thus we find anorexia and bulimia are prevalent in the fashion industry, dance, sport, executive wives etc.

### Possible causal effect factors . . .

(By Debbie Lovell, author of *Hungry for Love*)

When an individual develops an eating disorder, there are usually many factors which might be said to be involved in the cause. Eating disorders often develop at a stressful time, such as the time of important exams, or after a death or divorce.

Most cases of anorexia begin at or shortly after puberty, when the individual first encounters the developmental challenges of adolescence. The majority of bulimics develop their first symptoms slightly later, between the ages of sixteen and twenty.

Many sufferers come from families which place a high value on achievement. It is common for the parents of an anorexic to say she was a 'model child' who did what she was told and did not cause any bother.

The future anorexic or bulimic is generally someone who denies her own wants and needs, and seeks to please other people. She feels that she has to earn love and approval, and that her own needs are unimportant.

One factor which appears to be involved in virtually every case of anorexia, bulimia or compulsive eating is low self-esteem. If the individual had been able to accept herself as a person it is unlikely that she would have become so totally preoccupied with her appearance. Sufferers tend to lack self-confidence and to be unwilling to rebel outwardly.

Childhood experiences play a large part in the development of self-esteem. Those adults who have a reasonably healthy self-esteem are usually those who have been affirmed in childhood.

Some cases of eating disorders reveal a background of child abuse.

### Overcoming an eating disorder . . .

Many different types of treatment are available for people with eating disorders. The most effective seem to be those that deal with underlying problems, instead of focusing just on food and weight.

> *One factor which appears to be involved in virtually every case of anorexia, bulimia or compulsive eating is low self-esteem*

People with eating disorders often feel worthless, and long to be loved. Many people have recovered after discovering that God loves them and accepts them as they are, and that they are precious in His sight. God loves us whatever we look like, and He does not ask us to be perfect. All He asks is that we trust in Him, and receive His forgiveness. Jesus died so that we can be forgiven, and get rid of the burden of guilt which pulls us down. When we ask God to become central in our lives, every-thing else falls into perspective, and food and weight no longer seem so important. Recovery from an eating disorder takes time, but with God's help it is possible. I know because I myself recovered from anorexia. If you would like to know more about this, please contact Anorexia and Bulimia Care.

■ The above information is from Anorexia and Bulimia Care's web site which can be found at www.anorexiabulimiacare.co.uk

# Fighting Anna

**By Tess. Tess is 24 years old and was diagnosed
with anorexia two and a half years ago**

*'My illness developed as a result of a diet and exercise regime which snowballed into an obsession after I'd left university and started a full-time job. I received psychological treatment as an outpatient in an eating disorders unit of a hospital, I also took a course of anti-depressants to help me through the obsession. I now live and work in London and have a successful career in Marketing.'*

You don't 'get' anorexia like you get an illness. Anorexia is not an illness, it's a person. I call her Anna. Anna becomes you – your spirit and soul is shifted to one side whilst Anna comes to live inside your body with you. You're still in there too but Anna is stronger so you don't get a chance to show yourself very often until eventually you are completely silenced, and all everybody sees is your body with Anna living in it. And of course they think it's you – when it isn't – you're still there, trying to get back into your own body – fighting with Anna all the time. But she is always stronger.

I remember when she came to live in my body. I don't remember the exact day she arrived but I remember suddenly realising that the actions of my body were no longer my own, and wondering who it was that was making these decisions for me, and why I had to share my body with her. I was still strong then, I would tell Anna off when she tried to control me and I'd do what I wanted, ignoring her arguments. But it got to the point when after I'd eaten I'd weaken and then Anna would gain strength and make me feel so terrible that it was easier to let her choose when and what we ate. Of course, Anna hated food, and as she was in charge, I had to go with her choice of what to eat. Most of the time this was nothing. I would argue with her constantly – often shout and cry at her to leave me alone to eat what I wanted. But she'd never leave. This was hardest when I was out with my friends, or ready to eat with my family, because Anna would come with me but I couldn't argue with her in front of people because they didn't know she was there. So I lied. I had no other choice. Nobody else knew that Anna was there – they thought it was just me so how could I explain that Anna wouldn't let me eat when they didn't even know who she was? I couldn't. So I told them I wasn't hungry, or I was allergic to foods, or I felt ill. Anna would just sit there and laugh at me trying to convince everyone. It was okay for her, she lived in my body but couldn't feel my hunger, or my pain. She didn't care that my hair fell out, that my bones creaked or that my teeth were wobbling.

Eventually I ran out of lies, so I made sure I never had to be with people when they were eating or drinking. I just let Anna convince me to stay indoors alone – it was much easier that way and I was glad I didn't have to lie any more. People would talk about me – I knew why because I could see that my body looked wrong, that my bones were showing and my veins would stick out. I didn't like it – it was Anna's choice. It was her that got on the scales every day, and punished my body if another pound hadn't been knocked off. I wanted to tell everyone that it wasn't me that had done this – but how could I expect them to believe me when they didn't know about Anna?

And then I gave up the fight with Anna and I let her have my body to herself. I could no longer fight her and I felt that as my body was so useless now anyway, I didn't even want it any more. I would sit and watch while Anna controlled my body, masquerading as me whilst people sat and watched and talked about me as if I was the one refusing food and being hostile and rude. I resented them all. Had they just forgotten who I was? Did they just think I had turned into someone else? Did they not remember that I loved food and that I was fun and sociable?

There were a few people that knew it wasn't me. But they didn't know what Anna was doing, and whenever they tried to speak to me, they actually spoke to her and she answered so of course they couldn't

help me. They stuck by me though – well, they stuck by Anna thinking she was me which must have been hard for them because Anna was made of an evil that I can no longer comprehend. These people were my family. They were the ones that would eventually fight to get me back, and would eventually realise that they had to fight Anna to get to me. Though they didn't know it then. Back then they thought it was me.

People thought I didn't want to live any more. This wasn't true. I didn't want to share my body with Anna any more – and as she had claimed it as her own, this left me without one to live in. But at the same time, if I left, she wouldn't have wanted to be there without me. To anyone else this meant I wanted to die. That wasn't the case – I didn't want to die, but I would sooner have left my body than share it with Anna. And what other choice did I have? I resigned myself to the fact that there was no other way, and every day I waited for my body to give up and set me free. I felt it start to happen. First I lost my energy – I don't mean I felt tired – I lost the ability to walk more than a few feet before having to lie down. I had to summon all my strength just to go on breathing. My hair would come out in handfuls from my head and my nails had started to fall out. All the time Anna just watched and laughed – and I just waited. Knowing that soon it would all be over. Eventually I started to feel my heart flutter, trying to hold on though it was being burnt away with every breath I took. It was almost a relief knowing that soon I'd win over her – and that she couldn't survive without me.

Whether through fate, or for another reason, it was at this point that Anna showed herself to my family. Maybe she let it slip, or maybe it was because she knew she needed me. Whatever the reason they saw her and then everything changed. They said they knew I couldn't fight her on my own, but they said that together we'd be stronger, that we'd send her away, and that I could take my body back for myself. I didn't believe them. For two years I'd fought and fought. I'd watched her take my body and kill it slowly and painfully

while all I could do was sit by and watch. I'd seen her convince all of my friends that I'd done this to myself and eventually I'd surrendered to her knowing that I'd be dead, but at least I'd be free. How could I change that now? I didn't know how to eat food any more. I didn't know how to feel hunger any more. I didn't feel anything any more.

It took time for them to reach me. They had to fight her first, but eventually their voices came through and pulled me back and then I could help them fight her too. It took a long time for me to feel the strength to confront her – I had to concentrate more on giving my body the help it needed to go on living. It was a constant battle, with Anna trying to push me back every time I found a bit of strength. But this time there wasn't just me there to greet her. I had the strength of my family, and the doctors with their medication that gave me extra strength. Soon our combined powers were stronger than hers and we started to scare her off. She'd still creep up on me when I was alone, but I knew how to deal with her now.

---

*You don't 'get' anorexia like you get an illness. Anorexia is not an illness, it's a person. I call her Anna. Anna becomes you*

---

My body began to look normal again, and every day this gave me satisfaction because I knew that the stronger I got, the further away she was pushed. And then one day I woke up first, and had my first taste of life, albeit for just a few minutes, without her in my body. Then it was a few more minutes, then an hour, and then a whole day. When she wasn't there it wasn't like before she'd come into my life – it was better. Like the old proverb that says you don't know peace until you've experienced war, and you don't know happiness until you've felt sadness. Well, knowing how bad things could be with her there just made life even

better when she wasn't. Each day I felt her absence I knew I'd gained more strength to guard my body against her in the future.

That was a year ago. And now I look at my body and know that I control it. I won't lie and say she's not there, and I'm not blind to the fact that she is. But just as I was forced to sit and watch my body being controlled – so she is now. It's her that has had to surrender my body back to its rightful owner – me. And although occasionally I read her thoughts, or hear her voice, I have the power to push them away because my voice, and my thoughts are stronger. I don't know if she'll ever be totally gone. She may lie dormant beside me for ever. But now her being there serves a purpose. For as long as she's there, I will draw strength from her. For now she will only ever serve as a constant reminder that with the love and belief of my family's strength – and their belief in mine – I defeated her.

Anorexia can choose anyone's body to invade. At first it's hard to identify that it's not you, but her that is controlling you. After all, it's not every day we have to share our bodies unwillingly with another being. But once you know she's there, you can accept that it's not your fault that you're acting against your true will. Once you accept this, you can, with help, fight the other being living inside you. The most important thing to remember is that although many people will not understand that there is someone else using your body and killing your soul, someone will. And when that someone does, they can fight with you to get rid of the impostor. Don't ever let her win. I didn't let her win.

■ The above information is from the Eating Disorders Association. For help with eating disorders including anorexia and bulimia nervosa contact them at 103 Prince of Wales Road, Norwich, NR1 1DW. Tel: 0845 634 1414 (helpline open 8.30am to 8.30pm weekdays); 0845 634 7650 (youthline callers 18 and under – open 4.00pm to 6.30pm weekdays) E-mail: info@edauk.com Web site: www.edauk.com
© *Eating Disorders Association (EDA)*

# Risks

## Who is at risk for developing an eating disorder?

These disorders usually appear in bright, attractive young women between the ages of twelve and twenty-five, although there are both older and younger exceptions. At least ten per cent (10%) are male, possibly more. Researchers are just now beginning to determine how widespread eating disorders are in men and boys.

### Who is at risk for developing anorexia nervosa?

People who become anorexic often were good children – eager to please, conscientious, hard working, and good students. Typically they are people pleasers who seek approval and avoid conflict. They may take care of other people and strive for perfection, but underneath they feel defective and inadequate. They want to be special, to stand out from the mediocre masses. They try to achieve that goal by losing weight and being thin.

Some clinicians believe that the symptoms of anorexia are a kind of symbolic language used by people who don't know how to, or are afraid to, express powerful emotions directly, with words. For example, making one's body tiny and thin may substitute for, 'I'm not ready to grow up yet,' or 'I'm starving for attention.' Refusing to eat may translate to 'I won't let you control me!'

People who develop anorexia often feel stressed and anxious when faced with new situations. Many are perfectionists who have low tolerance for change (including the normal physical changes their bodies experience at puberty), feeling that it represents chaos and loss of control. Some set rigid, unrealistic standards for themselves and feel they have failed totally when they cannot achieve and maintain the degree of excellence they demand of themselves.

Although people with eating disorders don't want to admit it, many fear growing up, taking on adult responsibilities, and meeting the demands of independence. Many are overly engaged with parents to the exclusion of peer relationships. They use dieting and weight preoccupations to avoid, or ineffectively cope with, the demands of a new life stage such as adolescence, living away from home, or adult sexuality.

### Who is at risk for developing bulimia?

People who become bulimic often have problems with anxiety, depression, and impulse control (shoplifting, casual sexual activity, binge shopping, alcohol and drug abuse, and so forth). They do not handle stress gracefully. They may be dependent on their families even though they fiercely profess independence. Many have problems trusting other people. They have few or no truly satisfying friendships or romantic relationships.

They may diet, thinking to improve their lives and feel better about themselves. The deprivation leads to hunger, which leads to powerful cravings, which lead to binge eating. Feeling guilty, and afraid of weight gain, they try to remove calories from their bodies by vomiting, laxative abuse, fasting, or other methods of purging.

### Are some people at special risk?

Because of intense demands for thinness, some people are at high risk for eating disorders – wrestlers, jockeys, cheerleaders, sorority members, socialites, dancers, gymnasts, runners, models, actresses, entertainers, and male homosexuals.

*Because of intense demands for thinness, some people are at high risk for eating disorders*

### Eating disorders and physical or sexual abuse

Some clinicians find that a high percentage of their clients with eating disorders also have histories of physical or sexual abuse. Research, however, suggests that people who have been abused have about the same incidence of eating disorders as those who have not been mistreated. Nevertheless, the subject arises often enough to warrant discussion here.

People who have survived abuse often do not know what to do with the painful feelings and overwhelming memories that remain, sometimes even many years later. Some try to escape those feelings and memories by numbing themselves with binge food or through starvation. Some try to symbolically cleanse themselves by vomiting or abusing laxatives. Some starve themselves because they believe they are 'bad' and do not deserve the comfort of food and the nurture it represents.

As with all eating disorders, the starving and stuffing that follow abuse are coping behaviours. The key to recovery is finding out what the person is trying to achieve, or avoid, with the behaviours. S/he then needs to find, and use, healthier and more effective behaviours to feel better and make life happier. Almost always professional counselling is necessary to complete the process.

■ Please note: ANRED information is not a substitute for medical or psychological evaluation and treatment. For help with the physical and emotional problems associated with eating disorders, talk to your physician and a mental health professional.

■ The above information is from ANRED's web site which can be found at www.anred.com
© ANRED Anorexia Nervosa and Related Eating Disorders, Inc.

# Men get eating disorders too

## Information from the Eating Disorders Association

Eating disorders are illnesses that are generally believed to affect women rather than men. However, with more men now contacting Eating Disorders Association than in the past this raised the question of what treatment and services are available for them. Eating Disorders Association therefore commissioned a review of specialist healthcare provision across the UK for men with eating disorders and published the results in February 2000.

The overall findings identified a number of issues for men . . .

### Incidence and prevalence

- Gender and sexual orientation are significant factors.
- Approximately 10% of people with eating disorders are men and approximately 20% of men with eating disorders identify as gay, which is double the proportion of gay men in the population.

### Accessing services

- It is clear that the general lack of recognition of eating disorders in men makes it more difficult for them to access specialist eating disorder services. Their problems are less likely to be recognised and diagnosed by professionals including GPs and psychiatrists and therefore their illness may be well established before treatment is offered.
- Men find it hard to acknowledge they have an eating disorder and then to seek help. For example, weight loss is more likely to be attributed to physical causes rather than to psychological ones.

### How eating disorders develop

There is less cultural pressure on men to be slim although the 'sixpack' shape and image may be important. The onset of an eating disorder in men usually has a specific trigger.

These include:

- Avoiding childhood bullying/teasing for being overweight
- Bodybuilding/exercise
- Specific occupations including athletics, dance, horse racing etc.

A number of men with personal experience of eating disorders were interviewed in the course of preparing the report and some of their comments appear below.

The majority of the men reported that their eating disorders had started in their school years when they were overweight and called names. Several reported being severely overweight in their younger years, for a variety of reasons to do with low self-esteem, crises at home, and difficulties with coming to terms with their situation. For example, one man was 10 stone at 10 years and was put on a 'diet' by the school. This led to him eating on his own and being teased. However, some older men had experienced episodes of eating disorders throughout their lives, associated with loss of a partner, illness of a parent, a relationship breakdown, change of job, stresses of achieving higher university or work qualifications etc.

The particular pressures in the gay male community to have the 'body beautiful' and 'to be slim in order to get a partner' were mentioned by the gay men interviewed. Some gay men talked about the conflicts they had experienced when younger. It was felt to be a bigger problem in the gay male community than has previously been acknowledged. One man reported that his partner had helped him a lot. Men also experienced particular difficulty discussing their illness with their peers. One young man commented, 'It is more difficult to come forward, you cannot admit to your feelings in a macho culture; people think you are weak and you fear that you are going to lose respect from your friends.'

The men were asked about their experiences of treatment and care and identified the following issues as being particularly important: access to sympathetic professionals who did not moralise, who knew about eating disorders and who could provide specialist help.

Whilst some of the men interviewed had received a very prompt response from their GP, the general lack of recognition of the problem or the severity of it, by the GP and the consequent time it took to get specialist help, was a difficulty experienced by many people. GPs were seen as crucial, both because they often dealt with men on an ongoing basis and because they had the power to make appropriate referrals as well as to issue medical certificates.

■ The above information is from the Eating Disorders Association. For help with eating disorders including anorexia and bulimia nervosa contact them at 103 Prince of Wales Road, Norwich, NR1 1DW. Tel: 0845 634 1414 (helpline open 8.30am to 8.30pm weekdays); 0845 634 7650 (youthline callers 18 and under – open 4.00pm to 6.30pm weekdays) E-mail: info@edauk.com Web site: www.edauk.com

# Common misconceptions

**Below are some of the most commonly held misconceptions about the behaviours attributed to anorexia, bulimia and compulsive overeating**

*'I cannot be anorexic because I do eat when I have to . . .'*

Restriction of food and calories does not mean complete restriction for every sufferer. For some this means restricting certain types of foods (each individual sticking with what they perceive as 'safe foods') and limiting calories to below normal on a daily basis. For others this means fasting for a certain number of days and then eating 'normally' for the next number of days, and repeating the cycle continuously.

*'I don't fit any category . . . I only eat when I absolutely have to (but I don't binge) and then purge whatever I do eat . . .'*

Those suffering anorexia do not always completely restrict. Often when they cannot avoid a meal or food they will follow any consumption with self-induced vomiting or laxative abuse. This is considered 'Anorexia, Purging Type'. You should read the definitions of anorexia, bulimia, compulsive overeating, and binge eating disorder, as well as 'Eating Disorders not Otherwise Specified'.

*'I am above/on the high end of my healthy weight range . . . I cannot possibly have an eating disorder . . .'*

People suffering with any eating disorder can be of any weight. For most sufferers weight will continuously be going up and down. The weight of a person's body does not indicate their overall health, nor does it change the danger each sufferer may be in! There are more dangers involved in the disordered eating patterns themselves, rather than in each person's actual weight.

*'I eat a lot of candy, and can't possibly be anorexic . . .'*

Many anorexics and bulimics are junk-food addicts. There is little nutritional value to junk foods but they serve as a false sense of energy.

They also appease extreme cravings . . . for example, a sufferer's system may be depleted of sodium so there may be a strong craving for something salty. A bag of chips would seem to satisfy this craving. It is not uncommon to find a person with anorexia or bulimia who lives solely on candy (or junk-food), and like any eating disorder sufferer, this puts them in great danger. Other common 'replacements' are drugs, alcohol, coffee, tea and/or cigarettes.

*'Only middle-class, white teenagers suffer . . .'*

Anyone can suffer from anorexia or bulimia. Regardless of previously held beliefs, it is not only young, middle-class white teenagers or college students who can suffer. African-American, Hispanic, Asian, or white, women or men, rich to poor, from their teen years well into their fifties, there are sufferers from every age-bracket, class and culture. Don't rely on the 'written statistics' – they are based on reports made to government agencies and if a country, state, or province doesn't require that doctors report the cases, the statistics will not be accurate. Keep in mind as well, the more shame a person feels, the less likely that they will come forward and say they have an eating disorder . . . so if we keep perpetuating the idea that only 'young white women' suffer, more and more people who suffer that don't fit this ideal will not come forward, be acknowledged, and get the help they deserve.

*'I eat three meals a day (or I eat a lot during the course of a day) and never purge. How can I have an eating disorder? . . .'*

Disordered eating doesn't always mean restricting, binging and/or purging. Sufferers sometimes eat three meals a day, or eat continuously throughout the day and through this can deceive themselves into thinking that all is fine. If these eating patterns or meals consist of only lettuce, salad or yogurt (or other comparably low calorie, low fat food), and the calorie intake overall is far below normal (and is combined with emotional attributes), this would be considered anorexia. A person suffering may not be 'starving' themselves of food per se, but of any real calories, substance and nutrition. (The same is illustrated above in the example of eating candy.)

**'I don't make myself vomit or use laxatives, I cannot be bulimic . . . '**

There are other methods of 'purging' following a binge. The person suffering with bulimia will eat an unusually large quantity of food in a short period of time and follow it with purging; in addition to using laxatives or inducing vomiting, purging can also be compulsive exercise or complete fasting. This is one of the attributes that can be present in a person suffering both anorexia (restriction and purging without binging) and bulimia (binging and purging).

**'My family member/friend eats normally around me. He/She can't possible have an eating disorder . . . '**

It is not uncommon for those with anorexia, bulimia and compulsive Eating to eat 'normally' around others. This type of sufferer may look forward to their time alone, to be able to 'make up for' the time they've spent eating 'normally' around others. Anorexics will completely starve themselves, bulimics will binge and purge, and compulsive overeaters will overeat or binge once they have got back into their solitary environment. Sufferers may even look forward to being alone so they can partake in disordered eating patterns.

**'This is just a phase . . . '**

Anorexia, bulimia and compulsive overeating are not phases a child, teen or adult goes through. Some may go through dieting phases but this is far different from having an eating disorder. You should visit the other sections on the website to learn more about what having an eating disorder means.

**'I take vitamin/mineral supplements so I know I will stay healthy . . . '**

Vitamin supplements will not protect anyone from the harm an eating disorder will expose the body to. vitamins and minerals are absorbed into the body much more efficiently through their source food, and work in harmony with one another to ensure the highest level of

*Up to 30% of the sufferers of eating disorders (and maybe higher) will die as a result of a complication caused by the illness*

effectiveness and absorption. While taking vitamins and minerals may help to provide a sense of security, or even prolong certain aspects of health (like warding off infection), they will not protect you from the dangers associated with having an eating disorder, such as: the bowel or kidneys shutting down, shrinkage of the brain, dehydration, diabetes, TMJ Syndrome and misalignment of the teeth, tears in the aesophagus, ulcers, joint pain and arthritis, digestive and absorption problems, acid reflux disorders, cancer of the mouth and throat, low or high blood pressure, heart arrhythmia and cardiac arrest, loss of menstrual cycle, infertility, dilation of the intestines, or depression and suicide.

**'Everyone who is overweight or fat has compulsive overeating . . . '**

What defines the illnesses of compulsive overeating or binge eating disorder is more than just the weight range of the individual. Emotional eating, eating to fill a void, stuffing down feelings with binging, isolation and pushing others away are just some of the traits. There are also those who suffer from compulsive overeating or binge eating disorder who are not extremely overweight, as well, there are other reasons an individual can be overweight (including medical reasons or genetic predispositions to a larger body size). The overall symptoms that help determine if a person suffers from any disordered eating are how their eating relates to a lack of self-esteem and ability to cope with pain, anger and stress.

**'I can't die from this . . . '**

Anorexia, bulimia and compulsive overeating can kill those who suffer from them. Eating disorders have the highest rate of death out of any other psychological illness. Up to 30% of the sufferers of eating disorders (and maybe higher) will die as a result of a complication caused by the illness. Be sure to see the physical dangers sections to read about all the complications associated with anorexia, bulimia and compulsive overeating.

■ The above information is from the Something Fishy Website on Eating Disorders which can be found at www.something-fishy.org

# Women who go to extremes to lose weight

*By Emma Elms*

As Sarah*, 25, sat in her bedroom and removed a small piece of wire from the drawer beside her bed, she felt a familiar wave of excitement. She slowly placed the wire in her mouth and used it to scratch the back of her throat, overcome with relief that now her throat would be too sore for her to eat.

For several years, Sarah had been damaging her throat to stop her eating. This daily habit eventually gave her a ruptured blood vessel, but even that wasn't enough to make her stop.

Shocking as it is, Sarah's story is not unique. A worrying new trend is emerging among women suffering from Extreme Eating Disorders who are so desperate to be thinner they will try anything – however dangerous or irrational.

Some devour tissues or cotton wool to stop them feeling hungry. Others go as far as using syringes to remove blood (known as bloodletting) in the unfounded belief it can make them lose weight. Many take pills such as diuretics, which make them urinate more frequently and can damage the bladder.

Deanne Jade, head of the National Centre for Eating Disorders, who has been treating sufferers for 20 years, reveals that anorexic and bulimic women are employing increasingly desperate and violent methods to try to lose weight.

'An Extreme Eating Disorder is the escalation of a "normal" eating disorder such as anorexia or bulimia. When someone is alone and distressed, they can lose sight of what's dangerous and become unconcerned about the risk they are taking. Any extreme behaviour stemming from a desperate desire to be thin could be termed as an EED.'

There are around 1.1 million people with eating disorders in the UK, and 90 per cent of those are women, according to the Eating Disorders Association (EDA). What's more, statistics show eating disorders are on the rise: in 2000, some 19,000 sufferers called the EDA helpline, compared with just over 16,000 in 1999. An estimated one per cent of anorexics and bulimics have an EED – a figure which, according to the EDA, is increasing.

It's a worrying trend, made all the more so because of the extreme lengths sufferers will go to in a bid to control their weight, even down to draining away their own blood.

*Claire*, 34, who is bulimic, started draining blood from her own body three years ago in the hope it would help her lose weight.*
'As a teenager, I went through a phase of making myself sick after big meals because I was scared of getting fat, but I grew out of it,' she recalls. 'When I was 28 and working as a teacher, I moved into a flat in London. I became stressed and lonely and began taking out my frustration on food. Making myself sick after meals became a habit.

'I'd been a blood donor since the age of 18. When I was 31, I went to donate blood and told the nurse I was going swimming afterwards. She said: "You mustn't – it'll put too much stress on your body. It has to make up the blood it's lost".

'I felt so excited, thinking: "If I give blood, my body has to work harder, so I'll lose weight".'

A fortnight later, Claire, who now lives in Sheffield, attempted to give blood again but was told it was too soon.

'I decided if a nurse wouldn't remove the blood, I'd do it myself. I knew it was dangerous, but I was prepared to take the risk,' she says.

'I started using a syringe to remove blood from my arm. It really hurt, but afterwards I felt a sense of relief. Within a year I was removing a small jugful of blood about twice a week. Whenever I had a bingeing session, I'd remove blood, then be sick.'

Eventually Claire was referred to an eating disorders unit in a psychiatric hospital where her counsellor made her realise she has an obsessive personality and was dangerously anaemic. Today, her weight fluctuates between nine-and-a-half stones and ten stones, three pounds.

'Losing blood makes me feel weak and sometimes I pass out in the shower. It can take me an hour to get dressed as I have no energy,' adds Claire. 'Through reading medical journals, I've discovered it won't actually make me lose weight because it slows down my metabolic rate so my body can concentrate on making up the lost blood. But it's become an obsession.

'Last June, I saw a specialist who'd treated a woman with the same problem. When he told me she was dead, I was terrified. He warned me I'd be dead too before Christmas if I carried on, but I still can't stop.'

*Alice Harris*, 25, a recent graduate from north-west England, has suffered from anorexia and bulimia for 12 years. Three years ago she began using diuretic pills in a bid to lose weight.*
'They're meant for people suffering from water retention and help you

expel excess water,' she explains. 'I took the maximum dosage and soon found I needed to go to the loo every half-hour or so. It was inconvenient, but when the scales showed I'd lost a few pounds I felt proud.'

The pills quickly made her dehydrated and dizzy. 'I stopped taking the pills after six months because they made me feel so light-headed. I was disappointed to realise I wasn't losing fat, just fluid. I'd made myself ill for nothing.'

Most EED sufferers appear to share certain personality traits. 'Women with EEDs tend to be competitive, impulsive, withdrawn and lacking in social confidence,' explains Deanne Jade.

'Although this wasn't the case with Alice, many women with EEDs suffer from what is known as a "borderline personality disorder" where they can't cope with any strong emotions such as anger or hurt. They are consumed by those feelings and take out their frustration on food.'

Many sufferers may also have suffered some kind of trauma or abuse in their lives. 'Extreme Eating Disorders can develop as a reaction to a traumatic event,' says Jade. 'Sufferers might express this un-resolved pain from their past through abusing their bodies with food.'

Jade points out some of the methods used by women with EEDs are also forms of self-harm, a psychological illness that can be associated with eating disorders. 'A sufferer may start using a method such as letting blood or scraping the throat because they believe it is a way to lose weight or stop them-selves from eating. But then they experience a strange emotional high from it because it distracts them from their problems and temporarily releases their feelings of anger and anxiety,' she says.

'This is known as a "dis-associative activity" because feeling physical pain can stop sufferers feeling their emotional pain. Unlike the rest of us, they feel unable to deal with their problems in a different way.'

Dr Tony Jaffa, consultant psychiatrist at the NHS Phoenix Centre for young people with eating disorders, says that as sufferers become increasingly desperate to lose

## I was eating three man-size tissues every day

Annette Thorpe*, 33, has suffered from eating disorders, including bulimia, since her teens, and they have driven her to eat tissues and abuse laxatives.

She believes the trigger was her father's sudden death and the family's return to Britain from his RAF base in Cyprus.

'The change of lifestyle and onset of puberty made my weight go from eight to 11 stone in six months,' she recalls. 'When a friend confessed she made herself sick after meals, I was shocked, but the next night after dinner I sneaked upstairs and tried it. I felt excited to have found a way to lose weight. Soon I was making myself sick every day.

'A few months later, I developed a habit of chewing on a tissue. When I had a tissue in my mouth, I just didn't feel hungry. I would twist the end of a tissue, bite it off and swallow it. This stopped me wanting to eat and I started getting through a tissue a day, while still making myself sick after dinner every night.

'Within a couple of weeks, I was eating three man-size tissues a day, which I either nibbled or swallowed in chunks,' says Annette, who now lives in Lincolnshire.

'The side-effects were terrible. It made me really constipated and I'd get agonising stomach cramps. It was as if my whole system was blocked up, but it was the only way I could stop myself eating during the day. That year I lost one-and-a-half stone.'

Soon Annette began taking laxatives, both to lose weight and ease the constipation. She recalls: 'I went to the doctor, as whenever I was sick or went to the loo, I bled. He said I had Irritable Bowel Syndrome and that scared me into giving up eating tissues. When I was 20, my stomach cramps became so bad I had to give up the laxatives.

'Later that year, I finally admitted I had an eating disorder, although I still felt too embarrassed to tell anyone about the tissues.

'My weight has yo-yoed from six-and-a-half to eight-and-a-half stone. I still struggle to eat normally and I had a major relapse of anorexia and bulimia in January this year. As a result of eating tissues and taking laxatives, I still have continual stomach pains and have diarrhoea up to seven times a day. I can't believe I've wasted ten years abusing my body, but with the help of my new counsellor, I am determined one day I will recover.'

weight, they look for whatever means they can find – even though extreme methods, such as removing blood, will inevitably have serious health consequences.

'Blood-letting is extremely dangerous and could easily kill,' says Dr Jaffa. 'You could die from extreme blood loss and the strain it puts on the heart could lead to a heart attack.

'As blood isn't being pumped around your body properly, it could also cause fluid to accumulate on the lungs, stopping you from breathing. At the very least, it is likely to cause fainting, reduce your immunity to other illnesses and give you a nutritional deficiency.'

Other EEDs can also cause lasting damage. 'Eating substances such as tissue or cotton wool could cause a dangerous blockage in your digestive system,' says Dr Jaffa. 'It will undoubtedly stop your gastro-intestinal system working properly, leading to severe constipation and stomach pains.'

He emphasises the dangers of using diuretic pills unnecessarily. 'In my opinion, diuretic pills – even of the herbal variety – shouldn't be taken unless prescribed by a doctor.

'As they increase your need to urinate, they can dehydrate you very quickly. They also affect the balance of your blood chemistry, which could cause many of your bodily systems to fail.'

Sadly for Alice, the warning comes too late. 'It's nearly three years since I stopped taking diuretic pills, but my bladder has never recovered,' she says. 'I can't even make a car journey without stopping to use the toilet and my eating disorder has left me too weak to work.'

* Names have been changed.

© The Scotsman, November 2002

# Thin is not the answer

## Information from the Planned Parenthood Federation of America (PPFA)

Have you looked the other way when your friend goes to the bathroom too often? Do you envy the girl who lives on carrot sticks? You're not alone. We all keep very quiet about eating disorders. We wished we had them. We don't know how to get help. We fight shame, denial, guilt and fear. We don't even know what to say. But we can break the silence!

### What to do when you or your friend suffers over slenderness

*Get professional help*

The most important thing to know is that you can't heal yourself or your friend by yourself. No one can. If your friend refuses, remember that 'when a person is tired of dealing with the disorder, they'll want help,' according to Vivian Hanson Meehan, president of the American Association of Anorexia Nervosa and Associated Disorders (ANAD).

*Be gentle*

'Loving insistence from an important person can encourage earlier treatment,' Ms Meehan says. Know that this is not about food but about love. Let your friend know that you'll stand by her no matter what.

*Let a parent, teacher, or coach know about your concerns*

### What happens in treatment

When you suffer from anorexia or bulimia, both your heart and soul have to mend. Gradually, you'll learn to love and accept yourself. You'll discover new ways of nourishing yourself other than with food. But your body needs to heal just as much as your soul. You'll learn to eat normally again, without guilt. You'll start to learn that food and love are not the same thing. Successful treatment is always a team effort. It involves friends, family, support groups, a physician, and a nutritional therapist. Sometimes a psychotherapist, a psychiatrist, or a social worker is also needed.

*By Sophia Schweitzer*

### What recovery may feel like

Habits of starving and vomiting are terrifying to break. The anorexic inwardly dies with every pound that starts padding her featherweight frame. Her body image is so distorted that learning to feel beautiful is an enormous task. A bulimic needs to learn to feel fine with feeling full after a meal. Understanding that the craving to binge often strikes after a period of severe dieting, she needs to overcome a tenacious pattern of dieting, bingeing, and purging. Both

> *Thin is not the answer. You are lovable. But when you suffer, it takes time to learn that not everyone will hurt you and that you don't have to be perfect to be worthy of existence*

anorexic and bulimic teens need to learn to eat regular meals that include all the food groups.

Tell yourself or your friend it takes time. It isn't easy, and you can get better. No matter what. Thin is not the answer. You are lovable. But when you suffer, it takes time to learn that not everyone will hurt you and that you don't have to be perfect to be worthy of existence. It takes courage to be seen just as you are.

### How to prevent anorexia or bulimia

You're smart. You know dieting isn't really cool. Diets don't work. Instead, eat moderate amounts of anything that pleases you at least three times a day. (Include some vegetables and fruits.) Learn to feel good about yourself in other ways. And why not ask your school to start an educational programme, because too many of your friends are also at risk! ANAD can provide complete support.

■ The above information is from the Planned Parenthood Federation of America's web site which can be found at www.teenwire.com

# I think my friend may have an eating disorder

## What should I do?

In our food- and image-obsessed culture, it can be hard to tell whether someone has an eating disorder. It doesn't help that many of the actors on your favourite TV shows and the models in the magazines you read are extremely thin.

Lots of teens are critical of their bodies and lots of them diet or exercise to try to change them. Constantly talking about food and your body and striving to be skinny to fit into that bathing suit or prom dress can start to seem normal.

It crosses the line when a person starts to do things that are physically and emotionally dangerous and could have long-term health consequences. This could mean going on a starvation diet and getting down to an unhealthy weight (like with anorexia nervosa) or it could be bingeing and purging, either through forced vomiting, compulsively exercising, taking laxatives, or a combination (also known as bulimia nervosa). And although they're more common in girls, guys get eating disorders, too.

Other than dramatic weight loss, some signs that your friend may suffer from an eating disorder are:

- She has an obsession with weight and food – even more than general comments about how many calories she eats in a day. It seems like she never talks about anything else.
- She knows how many calories and fat grams are in everything that you and she eat – and she's always pointing them out.
- She works out compulsively – even when she's sick or exhausted.
- She avoids hanging out with you and her other friends during meals. For example, she avoids the cafeteria at lunch or the diner where you all hang out on weekends.
- She wears big or baggy clothes. (By itself, this may not be a symptom – lots of teens wear baggy clothes, but a teen who wears baggy clothes to conceal parts of her body she doesn't like isn't following a fashion trend.)
- She goes on severe diets, cuts food into tiny pieces, or moves food around on the plate instead of eating it.
- She goes to the bathroom a lot, especially right after meals, or you've heard her vomiting after a meal.
- She always talks about how fat she is, even though she's lost a lot of weight.
- She takes laxatives, steroids, or any other kind of diet pill.
- She has a tendency to faint, bruises easily, is very pale, or often complains of being cold (cold intolerance is a symptom of being at a dangerously low weight).

If your friend shows these symptoms and you're concerned, the first thing to do might be to tell her that you're worried, as gently as possible. Try to be a supportive listener. Of course, it's not your job to diagnose your friend – that's the job of a doctor who has been trained to make sure that what's going on is really an eating disorder and not something else. You're a good friend for wanting to help, and encouraging your friend to get medical care for what could be a dangerous situation is the best thing you can do for her. If she's willing to seek help, offer to go with her to talk to a counsellor or doctor.

Be as supportive as you can. You might also direct her to one of the many organisations, websites, hotlines, or other resources devoted to helping people who are battling eating disorders.

Avoid talking about food, trying to force her to eat, or reinforcing the idea that this is all about her physical appearance by telling her she 'looks sick' when she's dieting or 'looks good' when she gains some weight.

If your friend won't admit she has a problem, you need to get help from an adult you trust – her parents, your parents, a teacher, or a counsellor, for example. Eating disorders are serious, and they can cause permanent health problems or even death.

Trying to help someone who doesn't think she needs help can be like fighting an uphill battle – people who are in the midst of an eating disorder often have trouble admitting, even to themselves, that they have a problem. Because teens with eating disorders often have low self-esteem, the best thing you can do is be supportive and caring and let your friend know you care about her – no matter what she weighs.

■ This information was provided by KidsHealth, one of the largest resources online for medically reviewed health information written for parents, kids and teens. For more articles like this one, visit www.KidsHealth.org or else www.TeensHealth.org

© KidsHealth.org

# Carers' questions

## Some answers to questions carers/families frequently ask

***I am terrified of making the situation worse. How do I behave around my loved one? Should I behave normally or confront the situation?***

It is important for you to show warmth to the normal part of your daughter and to be able to maintain contact with that part of her. On the other hand you may need to set limits about the anorexic side which will depend on the severity, developmental age and degree of insight (see below). Remember to avoid coming on strong with power and confrontation (which sets things back in the opposite direction). You may need to roll with resistance, i.e. that sometimes it is worth agreeing to something small e.g. a rigid meal regime for the sufferer but then set limits for how many times a day the person must eat or how long a meal can take. Making the sufferer angry or upset because of setting limits with love (tough love) can't harm the sufferer.

***How can I encourage/make her seek help or visit the GP?***

It is important to get a good balance between avoiding conflict and confrontation. It will be helpful if you can make notes of what it is that you see that makes you worried.

You may have noticed problems such as:
■ Sensitivity to the cold
■ Hair becoming thinner
■ Mood becoming unstable
  Also talk about your feelings:
■ I am frightened about what I can see
■ I am confused and uncertain about what to do

It may then be helpful to set aside a time to discuss these things with your daughter and to give her the opportunity to express her point of view. You may need to have several meetings. If you are not able to get any agreed perspective you may need to resort to the concept of a higher power external to the family. Do this calmly and clearly without anger, criticism and sarcasm.

---

### On average it takes 6 years to recover from anorexia nervosa

---

'You have clearly expressed your point of view and I understand that you dismiss any of the concerns that I have raised. I do not think that either you or I have the expertise to make judgements about this. I know that in my role as your parent/partner/ sibling I am expected to be alert to things that can harm you and jeopardise your safety. From the things I have observed and told you about I think we may be in a dangerous situation. I know I would be expected to take my concerns to a doctor. I would like you to come with me so that you can put your point of view forward.'

***My child/loved one saw the GP who was very insensitive and unhelpful and caused a great deal of upset. What do I do now?***

You could return to your GP alone and discuss what happened and see whether you may be able to recover from this setback. If you think that the situation is irretrievable you could change GP.

***Mealtimes are very traumatic. How do I cope with these situations? Do I ignore the problem or address the situation?***

Meals are a time of hot emotion and so it is important that you have been able to develop strategies about what will happen in cooler planning meetings between meals.

There is no simple recipe about what should happen. You will need to have a problem-solving attitude to this. We always ask our adult

patients how they would like people to help them with meals. This can be tried and evaluated later. It may be that there need to be adjustments to the help given and accepted over time when the effectiveness of the help can be judged. Younger patients may not have the capacity to understand how they can be helped. However, it is useful if they are included in the planning stage. Again this needs to be discussed beforehand and evaluated at intervals.

The limits and boundaries are clear. There is legislation in this country, which ensures that no individual can put his or her life in danger because they have anorexia nervosa. Therefore if the anorexia nervosa is so severe such that the help at home is insufficient then more intensive care such as day patient or inpatient treatment is required. If necessary this may need to be given on an involuntary basis using the Mental Health Act.

*I think that my child may have an eating disorder. I am very worried about them. How do I broach the subject?*
This question relates to the first one. There is a detailed discussion of this issue in *Anorexia Nervosa: A Survival Guide* and in the book from Great Ormond St. It may be helpful for you to gradually compile a list of all the signs that you observe that make you think your child has an eating disorder. The books may be helpful in that they can help you focus on what to look out for. Then arrange to have a quiet conversation about these issues.

*My daughter is undertaking a range of treatment approaches including motivation enhancement therapy, drama therapy, art therapy and occupational therapy. What are these different therapies and what do they aim to achieve?*
One of the aims of therapy is for the individual to be able to reflect clearly on his or her mind (thoughts, emotions, drives etc.) and to understand its strengths and weaknesses and to be able to work with it for optimal function. These various treatments use different strategies for

reaching this understanding. For some people using words and talking treatment is important. For others, using movement or other forms of expression can help emotional understanding and processing. It is not easy to predict what will work, when and for whom. Often for severe cases such as those which require inpatient treatment a variety of strategies are used.

*How long does it take to recover from an eating disorder? Is a full recovery from an eating disorder really possible?*
On average it takes 6 years to recover from anorexia nervosa. The degree of recovery varies and many people are left with traces of the vulnerability towards weight and food. Research with people who have made a full physical recovery in terms of weight gain and reproductive function shows that there are residual abnormalities in the stress response. It is uncertain whether such abnormalities preceded the illness and were part of the risk factor to develop the illness or whether they are a scar from the illness.

*My daughter's eating disorder is having a very disruptive and distressing effect on the family and is detracting attention from my other children and partner. What suggestions can you make for dealing with this situation?*
This is a common problem and it is difficult for any family to do this sort of multi-tasking. Try to make plans to timetable enjoyable shared

activities with all members of the family. Have your strategies for dealing with meals worked out in advance and have time limits and boundaries about the help given to combat the anorexia help. Ask for help from friends and family.

*I find the constant pressure and tension of living with someone with an eating disorder is beginning to affect my health. What suggestions can you make to help with this situation? How can I continue to manage?*
Research has found that most people who care for someone with an eating disorder experience high levels of distress. This can even reach the levels of clinical syndromes such as anxiety and depression. It may be that medication can help reduce the intense arousal levels that can paralyse effective action. The important thing will be to try to get both emotional and practical support both from your informal network of friends and family but also from professionals, i.e. your GP or social services. Set yourself reasonable goals and use problem-solving strategies to cope. What we have found is that the distress is most acute in those who experience the most positive aspects of the relationship with their child and are aware of the loss caused by the illness.

■ The above information is from King's College London's web site which can be found at www.iop.kcl.ac.uk

*© King's College London*

# Eating disorders can be prevented!

*By Michael Levine, PhD and Margo Maine, PhD*

### What is eating disorders prevention?

Prevention is any systematic attempt to change the circumstances that promote, initiate, sustain, or intensify problems like eating disorders.

- Primary prevention refers to programmes or efforts that are designed to prevent the occurrence of eating disorders before they begin. Primary prevention is intended to help promote healthy development.
- Secondary prevention (sometimes called 'targeted prevention') refers to programmes or efforts that are designed to promote the early identification of an eating disorder – to recognise and treat an eating disorder before it spirals out of control. The earlier an eating disorder is discovered and addressed, the better the chance for recovery.

### Basic principles for the prevention of eating disorders

- Eating disorders are serious and complex problems. We need to be careful to avoid thinking of them in simplistic terms, like 'anorexia is just a plea for attention', or 'bulimia is just an addiction to food'. Eating disorders arise from a variety of physical, emotional, social, and familial issues, all of which need to be addressed for effective prevention and treatment.
- Eating disorders are not just a 'woman's problem' or 'something for the girls'. Males who are preoccupied with shape and weight can also develop eating disorders as well as dangerous shape control practices like steroid use. In addition, males play an important role in prevention. The objectification and other forms of mistreatment of women by others contribute directly to two underlying features of an eating disorder: obsession with appearance and shame about one's body.
- Prevention efforts will fail, or worse, inadvertently encourage disordered eating, if they concentrate solely on warning the public about the signs, symptoms, and dangers of eating disorders.

> *Eating disorders arise from a variety of physical, emotional, social, and familial issues, all of which need to be addressed for effective prevention and treatment*

Effective prevention programs must also address:

- Our cultural obsession with slenderness as a physical, psychological, and moral issue.
- The roles of men and women in our society.
- The development of people's self-esteem and self-respect in a variety of areas (school, work, community service, hobbies) that transcend physical appearance.
- Whenever possible, prevention programmes for schools, community organisations, etc., should be coordinated with opportunities for participants to speak confidentially with a trained professional with expertise in the field of eating disorders, and, when appropriate, receive referrals to sources of competent, specialised care.

- The above information is from the National Eating Disorders Association's web site which can be found at www.NationalEatingDisorders.org

CAUSES OF EATING DISORDERS
- PHYSICAL
- EMOTIONAL
- FAMILIAL ISSUES

# Body image

## Information from the National Centre for Eating Disorders

**B**ody image is a fact of life, we all have opinions about our bodies – and we all experience a greater or lesser degree of self-esteem. These are separate aspects of something we all desire – self-confidence. People with poor self-esteem could feel relaxed about their appearance; however, it is unlikely that people with poor body image would feel good about themselves.

There are several dimensions to how we view our bodies. We all, for example, have subjective opinions about how we look: how old or young, fat or thin, how big or small – even how beautiful or ugly we are. We might compare ourselves to other people in areas which are important to us. And we are not immune from wondering how other people see us, we usually assume that they see us exactly as we see ourselves.

These perceptions and beliefs about our bodies will provoke feelings which may be positive or negative, proud or ashamed, or perhaps we don't have many feelings about our bodies at all.

Our emotional reactions to the way we believe we look can have profound effects on the way we behave. Intense feelings about our appearance can lead us to make adjustments in our lifestyle to compensate or cope with how we feel about our bodies. We find ourselves doing certain things, like dressing up to attract attention, or only wearing black. Alternatively if our bodies are a source of embarrassment or shame we may hide away, refuse to do exciting things like buy new clothes or engage in fun-filled activities and this could make us quite depressed.

It can be hard for us to make a distinction between our subjective perceptions of our bodies and the way we really look. As a result, most

*By Deanne Jade*

men and women are dissatisfied with some aspect of their appearance such as the size of their thighs or the wrinkles on their face, even if they have proof that the way that they feel on the inside does not stand up to tests of reality.

We think that this is due to the pervasive influence of the media, TV, cinema and fashion magazines. We are being continually bombarded with images and messages telling us how we are supposed to look and what we are supposed to do to achieve it, through diet, exercise and many other things. If you can look the way the media tell you to, you can have permission to feel good about yourself, if not you must try harder. These pressures bear heavily on women who have a greater degree of body insecurity than men because, since time began, women have been valued for how they look while men have been valued for what they can

achieve. But our society is also influencing men; we see this reflected in the increasing numbers who go to the gym, who adjust their eating habits in pursuit of the perfect body shape and who may even resort to surgical enhancement of their looks.

> *Our society is also influencing men; we see this reflected in the increasing numbers who go to the gym, who adjust their eating habits in pursuit of the perfect body shape*

The trouble is that ideal images change from time to time and we cannot change our bodies quite so readily to suit the fashion of the day. This creates a lot of anxiety especially among people who are emotionally vulnerable and who spend a lot of time comparing

themselves to others. In such cases looking 'wrong' can be just one more reason to dislike ourselves.

Anxiety and worry about the body, without the protective influence of high self-confidence, can provoke strange behaviours which are at the least uncomfortable and distressing, such as engaging in obsessional exercise routines or declining to have a normal social life. But at the very worst these behaviours can be damaging – such as happens when people adopt dangerous eating behaviours, or use drugs to control their weight. If people stop to examine their habits and routines, they are often surprised to discover just how much fear of body exposure has gradually created limitations in their lives. As an example, the annual orgy of dieting that many people engage in prior to taking their summer break (fearing the blast of disapproval at the beach!) gives testimony to how deeply ingrained is the national fear of being physically judged.

---

*Poor body image can unwittingly trap a person in a cycle of depression and low self-worth from which it is difficult to escape*

---

Of course, if we allow negative body feelings to limit our lives too much, we are bound to feel even worse about ourselves, and the more likely we are therefore to blame the size, shape or appearance of our body. Thus, poor body image can unwittingly trap a person in a cycle of depression and low self-worth from which it is difficult to escape.

Body opinions need to be separated from cultural pressures to look a certain way. Most people can adjust their thinking with just a little guidance; they accept that life is not a rehearsal and they learn to deal with their anxiety, they go out and enjoy life however they look. But some people find it hard to switch off

their internal critic and they are driven to continue abusing themselves. Such people may need professional assistance in the form of counselling or psychotherapy to improve their self-esteem.

Our genes predict our looks before we are born. It can take a lot of work to make any meaningful difference, and the best we can become is more a question of caring for ourselves than of beating ourselves into shape. Our bodies are, after all, the only means we have of experiencing the sensual and emotional joys of our world. Body confidence and self-acceptance go hand in hand with self-esteem, and are the only route to a full and rewarding quality of life.

*© National Centre for Eating Disorders 2003*

---

# Body image

## Information from the National Eating Disorders Association

### Body image is . . .

- How you see yourself when you look in the mirror or when you picture yourself in your mind.
- What you believe about your own appearance (including your memories, assumptions, and generalisations).
- How you feel about your body, including your height, shape, and weight.
- How you sense and control your body as you move. How you feel in your body, not just about your body.

People with negative body image have a greater likelihood of developing an eating disorder and are more likely to suffer from feelings of depression, isolation, low self-esteem, and obsessions with weight loss.

We all may have our days when we feel awkward or uncomfortable in our bodies, but the key to developing positive body image is to recognise and respect our natural shape and learn to overpower those negative thoughts and feelings with positive, affirming, and accepting ones.

*Accept yourself – accept your body*
*Celebrate yourself – celebrate your body*

### Negative body image is . . .

- A distorted perception of your shape – you perceive parts of your body unlike they really are.
- You are convinced that only other people are attractive and that your body size or shape is a sign of personal failure.
- You feel ashamed, self-conscious, and anxious about your body.
- You feel uncomfortable and awkward in your body.

### Positive body image is . . .

- A clear, true perception of your shape – you see the various parts of your body as they really are.
- You celebrate and appreciate your natural body shape and you understand that a person's physical appearance says very little about their character and value as a person.
- You feel proud and accepting of your unique body and refuse to spend an unreasonable amount of time worrying about food, weight, and calories.
- You feel comfortable and confident in your body.

■ For more information, contact the National Eating Disorders Association at 603 Stewart St, Suite 803, Seattle, WA 98101 Web site: www.NationalEatingDisorders.org

*© 2003 National Eating Disorders Association*

# The fat of the land

## We're getting fatter because we've forgotten how to enjoy food

The girl on the StairMaster pounds the steps, her breath short and sharp, her face red with exertion. A sweaty T-shirt clings to her – and even through the cotton you can make out the ridges of her spine. She is emaciated. Dark hair covers every inch of her skeletal arms. It hurts to look at her.

Equally, it hurts to look at the man beside her. He too stands on the StairMaster, but the size of him means that you can hardly see the machine beneath his vast body. He breathes with difficulty, and sweat pours off him, soaking the rolls of T-shirt that encase his torso. As in my gym, so in life. While the alarm was raised this week about 75 per cent of Britons being obese by 2020, an epidemic of young women suffering from anorexia is also sweeping the land: one in 10 girls under 21 have been diagnosed with anorexia. Both trends reveal our unhealthy relationship with food.

The staff of life has become the stuff of nightmare. Where once upon a time meals were celebrations of family closeness, individual well-being, religious rituals, today most people view food with fear: lest it make us fat, ill, lose time, smell funny, look different from everyone else. Fewer than 40 per cent of Britons claim to sit down at a table for meals; fewer than 30 per cent cook all their own meals.

Watch people on a Tube platform or on the high street: some will be swigging from a soft-drink can, some nibbling a chocolate bar, others scoffing a burger. Food (and drink) punctuate their walk, talk and gestures – linking, like a comma or a colon, different moments. No matter that cookery shows beef up our television schedule; or that celebrity chefs hog our newspapers. The unpalatable truth is that most Britons view food with either indifference or suspicion. No wonder. Food has become confusing in a culture that peddles simultaneously a slimline

By Cristina Odone

aesthetic and the fast food, television, video games and other sedentary leisure activities which guarantee this enviable 'look' won't be achieved.

---

*Eat junk food and you risk obesity – with its attendant increase in the chances of contracting diabetes, cancer and heart disease*

Obesity, according to Susie Orbach, author of *Fat Is a Feminist Issue* and *On Eating*, 'is a response to people feeling attacked in their bodies'. On television, movies, magazines 'model' men and women with perfectly trim, wonderfully toned bodies smile back at you: the frustration of not measuring up prompts you to reach for comfort

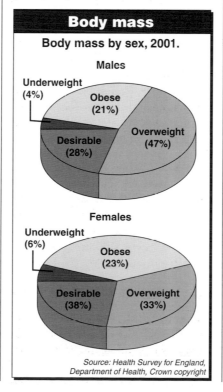

**Body mass**

Body mass by sex, 2001.

Males

Underweight (4%)
Obese (21%)
Overweight (47%)
Desirable (28%)

Females

Underweight (6%)
Obese (23%)
Overweight (33%)
Desirable (38%)

Source: Health Survey for England, Department of Health, Crown copyright

food. In the face of constant – even if unspoken – criticism about your weight, a chocolate binge or a feast of jam doughnuts is tantamount to sticking two fingers up at the body fascists out there. Anorexics, instead, see food as a four-letter word that threatens to pollute their pure, unadulterated little-girl (or, more infrequently, little-boy) world. Both groups, as Susie Orbach points out, inevitably go hungry – and needy. A society composed of these dissatisfied citizens – the bag of bones, the grossly fat – has little to recommend it.

Somewhere between this polarity of response lies a balanced diet of five portions of fruit and veg, a bit of protein, a few carbohydrates. But this is no longer the staple fare; you're far more likely to be stuffing your face with a Big Mac or a Kentucky Fried Chicken wing. (Around the world, McDonald's boasts 45 million customers daily.)

In *Fast Food Nation*, American journalist Eric Schlosser condemns those fast-food industrialists who, with a beady eye on the profit margin, ignore the effect their food has on our health. Cheap to make, oozing fat, high in salt, sugar and God knows what additives, fast food emerges as the primary culprit in our criminal abuse of our bodies. Eat junk food and you risk obesity – with its attendant increase in the chances of contracting diabetes, cancer, heart disease.

More sinister still, as Schlosser shows, fast-food marketing men have seized upon children as 'brand-loyal, from cradle to grave': they target the under-eights with Disneyesque mascots, cartoon strips and related accessories, and bank on the child's loyalty for ever more – or until his first heart attack.

Is the Government defending our interests in the battle of the flab? No, warns Profesor Philip James, co-author of a report on obesity which was presented at a EU meeting in Copenhagen last week. 'Officials are pretty terrified about how to confront some of the vested interest.' The same government that restricted tobacco advertising and hiked up prices on cigarettes and alcohol, could make mincemeat of food and soft-drink giants. Banning soft-drink vending machines from schools, reviewing fast-food advertising, increasing the price of the more nefarious processed food products: there are many ways for Labour to curb our appetite for the unhealthy.

But big business not only threatens our health, it also shapes our body image. From the diet company that flaunts the before and after pictures of a tubby housewife transformed into a lithe glamour puss, to the television programme makers whose stars are all perfect size 10s, physical conformity is being pushed down our throats.

Some experts are finding this indigestible. Last January, Susie Orbach launched a campaign called 'Anybody' which aims to reshape our view of ourselves – so that we can accept that within the canon of beauty, diversity is a plus. Fat, thin, plump, scrawny: Orbach and others hope that one day we will realise we are worth more than our weight in pounds and ounces. Maybe one day, my gym will be full of men and women of average size, pounding away on their StairMaster in between two healthy meals enjoyed at the kitchen table. Maybe one day.

Cristina Odone is deputy editor of the *New Statesman*.

■ This article first appeared in *The Observer*, 25 September 2002.
© *Guardian Newspapers Limited 2002*

# Young girls who think they are too fat to be perfect

### By Beezy Marsh, Medical Reporter

Girls as young as seven risk developing eating disorders because they think they are too fat, a study has found.

Images of very thin celebrities such as Geri Halliwell, Victoria Beckham and *Ally McBeal* actress Calista Flockhart are thought to encourage a desire to be thin, even in the youngest children.

The study found almost half of girls between seven and 12 wanted to be slimmer. Just over one in three boys in the same age group said they wanted to lose weight.

The study, carried out by psychologists at Surrey University and Melbourne University, Australia, provides alarming evidence that poor body image – a factor in harmful dieting – begins well before puberty.

Experts writing in the *British Journal of Clinical Psychology* said media images which portray ultra-slim bodies as the most desirable probably influence very young children's desire to be thin.

Psychologist Dr Helen Truby, who led the study, said: 'It is surprising how many young children are aware of their body shape and size at such an early age.

'It was believed children didn't develop an adult ideal until puberty. But children at seven are aware whether they are satisfied with their bodies.'

The study of 312 youngsters is the first to test children's preference for different bodies based on body mass index, a measure used by doctors to define obesity.

Doctors calculate BMI by dividing a patient's weight in kilograms by height in metres squared.

A BMI of more than 25 in adults is classed as overweight and more than 30 is obese.

Dr Truby, of Surrey University, and colleague Dr Susan Paxton, from Melbourne, measured the BMI of each child before photographing them to identify their 'range' of body sizes.

From these photographs a series of seven 'body figures' were generated – one set each for girls and boys to represent the range of BMIs.

The children were then asked to identify which 'body figure' was most like their own – their perceived figure – and which they would most like to have – their ideal figure.

Forty-eight per cent of girls selected an ideal body figure thinner, 42 per cent a figure the same size and only 10 per cent larger than their perceived figure.

Thirty-six per cent of boys selected a thinner ideal body figure, 44 per cent the same size and 20 per cent a larger figure. Neither boys nor girls wished to have a figure in the higher BMI categories.

'Our findings lend support to the view children develop cultural concepts of desirable physical attributes particularly related to body thinness well before puberty,' said Dr Truby.

'The consequences to public health of these findings in relation to the desire for a thin body, which is relatively unachievable for most children, needs careful consideration.'

She warned that there was a danger that vulnerable children could indulge in 'extreme dieting behaviour'.

Sarah Schenker, of the British Nutrition Foundation, said the findings were worrying.

'If children are tempted to try to lose weight they risk nutrient deficiency which could hinder both mental and physical development.

'They may start tying to exclude key foods such as dairy produce or bread, when a healthy, balanced diet, combined with physical activity is what they need.'
© *The Daily Mail June, 2002*

# Don't put your daughter on a diet

**Not even if she's overweight. And not even a 'moderate' diet. Unless you want to increase her risk of developing an eating disorder**

*By Kate Fox, Co-Director, Social Issues Research Centre (SIRC)*

According to a study published recently in the *British Medical Journal*, adolescent girls who diet even 'moderately' are five times more likely to become anorexic or bulimic than those who do not diet. Those on strict ('severe') diets are eighteen times more likely to develop an eating disorder.

While it is always unwise to over-react to the results of a single study, and other psychological and social factors are clearly involved in the development of eating disorders, these findings are nonetheless worrying, and it is therefore surprising that only two major media sources reported this story (the Health section of the BBC News website and *The Guardian*). Even those who did give it a brief mention emphasised the value of exercise as much as the dangers of dieting.

This uncharacteristic squeamishness (imagine the banner headlines if, say, GM foods had been similarly 'linked' to anorexia) could be due to the fact that the *British Medical Journal* study is 'off-message' in terms of the current health orthodoxy, in which obesity and overweight are regarded as the main public health problems, and low-fat, 'healthy' diets as the miracle cure. Monitoring the media, one cannot help noticing that current 'health promotion' messages disseminated by government agencies and health charities are often virtually indistinguishable from the propaganda of the multi-million-pound slimming/diet industry. Both make the basic (mistaken) assumption that slim = healthy, and both often adopt the same scare-tactics and moralistic tones.

Rather than expressing concern about the ways in which the slimming industry exploits and preys on the anxieties of vulnerable adolescent girls, persuading them that the perfectly natural and healthy weight and fat gains of puberty are a 'problem', the health establishment, by focusing campaigns exclusively on the dangers of overweight and dietary fat, is tacitly condoning this message.

## Those on strict ('severe') diets are eighteen times more likely to develop an eating disorder

Pick up any slimming or diet magazine (almost all of which are produced by slimming-club chains), and you will find the word 'health' or 'healthy' on every other page. Those advertising diet products and slimming aids are also jumping on the health bandwagon. While the health educators continue to tout the simplistic message that any degree of overweight is unhealthy, and imply that losing weight is automatically a healthy thing to do, they can hardly object to the cynical slimming industry joining them on the moral high-ground.

Health professionals should take note, however, of the growing body of research evidence showing that the majority of normal-weight and even underweight adolescent girls already believe that they are too fat, and that increasing numbers are dieting, to the detriment of both their physical and mental health.

We are of course by no means the first scientists to express concern about over-zealous promotion of weight loss by the health establishment. In January 1998, to take just one prominent example, the editors of the *New England Journal of Medicine* asked: 'Given the ambiguous benefits of weight loss, why are physicians and public health officials joining in the general enthusiasm for losing weight?' They suggested that 'the medical campaign against obesity may have to do with a tendency to medicalize behavior we do not approve of' and accused health professionals of 'overstating the dangers of obesity and the redemptive powers of weight loss'.

The *New England Journal of Medicine* urged health professionals to speak out against the public's excessive infatuation with being thin and help the public regain a sense of proportion. This advice, it seems, has been ignored.

(Note: The Social Issues Research Centre is conducting a review of the research literature on dieting and eating disorders. This study is currently in the early stages, but an overview will be published on their web site when the research is completed.)

# You are not a model, you are a real person!

**Are you dressing to impress?**

Well, if you are a female person of our society then of course you are, that's what girlies do!!

But hang on a mo, do you buy the latest design of cropped trousers because they look good on Naomi Campbell or because they look good on you and you feel com-fortable?

To look good I believe you need to feel good as well, and you need to be yourself and be happy with who you are, however, there is a growing problem that many young girls out there are trying too hard to be like their role models.

To find out more about models and how their looks can influence other young girls, read on.

Everyone likes to look good, why not, we can then feel good about ourselves, and we may even be lucky enough to attract someone of the opposite sex! The problems start when we look in the mirror and we see something that we don't want to see, yes I know a big red spot on your forehead, no, it's when we are unhappy with the way we look. Many factors can be the trigger of these feelings

### Catalogues

*Picture this*: You are looking through your catalogue in the hope of finding something sparkly and spangly to wear out next weekend for your best bud's birthday 'night out', you flip over the page and finally find something that you think you like, then you stop and look at the girl who's modelling your dress, how do you feel?

*Answer*: Before you began looking at the catalogue you probably felt really excited and motivated towards buying something for your bud's night out, but when someone else is modelling your dress, it suddenly seems less appealing. Research has shown that girls'

motivation levels can easily be destroyed by simply showing them pictures of models.

### Big is beautiful

However, I think that if young girls were to see 'everyday' girlies modelling their clothes, like your average next-door neighbour, then people would feel more relaxed and comfortable. It is very off-putting to find that your newly bought black dress looks better on Victoria Beckham than it does on you. False images are a bad thing and I feel that we girlies are given false hopes, but don't worry girls it's simply advertising to earn money and just imagine what poor old Posh Spice looks like when she gets up in the morning (it's a horrible thought!!) but no one looks great in the morning do they?

### Eating the right kinda food

Eating is a way for our body to function, so we need to eat something, and we all know that we never eat healthily 100% of the time, but when we start to eat nothing at all we then need help.

### Why do people turn to a no-food diet?

When we look at models they seem to have long white faces that look tired and unwell, their bodies are barely visible and they have no definite shape or structure. Is this the image that advertisers want to convey? Is this what we want young people to believe is the right way to be in order to look good and be successful?

This is wrong, everyone is who they are and who they want to be, and images like this encourage young girlies to feel that this is the right way. As a result the only way to look as good as the models (do they really look good?) is to eat nothing. This eating disorder is known as anorexia and it is a growing problem in many young girls. Ideas on how to eat healthily can be found on other pupiline web pages.

Images of models can be found everywhere that we look, and I think that these images need to be changed to create a better lifestyle for young people, especially us girlies.

Every young female out there reading this must be proud of who you are, if everyone was the same the world would be terribly boring and there would be no good looking blokes to swoon over!!! Being an individual is important and models whatever shape or size will never be you, and you will never be them, so be happy and enjoy being you!

## Question

When I look in magazines and see these models I think, I want to be like her with her golden hair, blue eyes and not one spot, I feel so down, every other page in the magazine is plastered with faces of pretty girls!

## Answer

Everyone is pretty in his or her own way, and you must not think that to be pretty you need to be a model. In everyday life every teenage girl will experience their

first outbreak of spots, this is bad, I know but everyone is in the same boat. Models can't rule your life, be yourself.

Models are an image and they are not real, they are just made to perfection and this is not the human race, this is how we want people to be, but we cannot control what we look like, as we can food. You need to enjoy life as you, there is no harm in wanting to look good, but if you feel that you are not eating and you see that being thin is the right way to be then please contact the organisations listed at the back of this book.

Remember. You are loved and liked for who you are, not for what you look like. So eat healthily and shop till ya drop!!!!

■ The above information is from Pupiline's web site which can be found at www.pupiline.net

# Body image and eating disorders

## Information from the British Nutrition Foundation (BNF)

The government has asked the broadcasting standards commission to evaluate whether a sufficiently diverse group of women appear as presenters and guests on television. The monitoring is designed to address growing concerns that images of excessively thin models in magazines and on television have led to an increase in eating disorders.

A recent study on body image, eating disorders and the media by the British Medical Association found that many models and actresses, who are commonly cited as popular role models by young girls, have 10-15% of their body composition as fat whereas the average proportion of body fat for a healthy woman is between 22-26%.

A recent government survey reporting on the diets of British schoolchildren found that one in six girls aged 15-18 years were dieting to lose weight. The survey also found that this age group was most likely to have poor intakes of a number of vitamins and minerals, including vitamin D, iron, calcium and zinc.

Anorexia and bulimia nervosa are debilitating diseases, which can be fatal. In most cases the disease results in a poor nutritional status that can increase the risk of secondary diseases such as osteoporosis and heart disease. The treatment of these conditions requires a multi-disciplinary approach as the causative factors are extremely complex.

Anorexia and bulimia can be triggered by a life event. Sufferers use excessive slimming and

exercising as a way of controlling certain aspects of their lives, at a time when they feel unable to control other events.

It must also be recognised that obesity and overweight are increasing rapidly in the UK population. Being obese and overweight is associated with increased risk of heart disease, cancer, stroke and diabetes mellitus; these are currently the leading causes of death in Britain. While it is prudent to be aware of the pressures that images of extremely thin women can have on vulnerable young girls, it is also crucial that support and education is provided for those who are overweight and wish to achieve a healthy body weight.

■ The above information is from the British Nutrition Foundation's web site which can be found at www.nutrition.org.uk Alternatively, see page 41 for their address details.

# Image obsession

## Image obsession that means one woman in four is always dieting

The number of women on a diet has doubled in the past 15 years. One in four is restricting her food intake at any one time in an attempt to slim down.

Yet while the nation appears obsessed with weight and image, the healthy eating message is still being ignored, according to nutrition experts.

Britons persist in consuming vast amounts of fast food – and not nearly enough fruit and vegetables.

Then they try to undo the damage with a cocktail of vitamin and mineral supplements. There has been a surge in the numbers popping such pills, up from 17 to 40 per cent.

> **The number of women on a diet has doubled in the past 15 years. One in four is restricting her food intake at any one time in an attempt to slim down**

The picture of a misguided nation chomping its way though mountains of junk food then seeking solace in yo-yo diets, food fads and supplements, emerged in the *National Diet and Nutrition Study*.

Yesterday, the Food Standards Agency said these were not solutions for those who routinely consume foods high in fat, sugar and salt.

It advised women to eat a diet which balances consumption with activity and said taking pills was unnecessary.

The Government, through the FSA and the Department of Health, has spent millions of pounds trying to get healthy eating messages across. It doesn't seem to have worked.

Average consumption of oily fish is just one-third of the recommended single portion a week.

Fruit and vegetables fare no better. The average is 2.7 portions a day for men and 2.9 for women – compared to a recommended figure of five.

One in five men eats no fruit at all in a week, while 15 per cent of women also fall into this category. No men routinely eat five portions a day.

Young men are eating no more fruit and vegetables today than they did 15 years ago, while the picture is little better for women.

Families living on benefits are much less likely to eat fruit and vegetables. Women in this group also consume more chips, burgers, kebabs, meat pies and full-fat milk.

The idea that we pile on the pounds only to lurch into a diet is demonstrated by the fact that the proportion of women trying to lose weight has risen from 18 to 24 per cent since 1987. For men, the figure climbed from 4 to 10 per cent.

Alette Weaver from the FSA said older people who eat traditional meals, with meat and three vegetables, had a much healthier diet.

'Young people are far more likely to eat on the go, things like burgers, kebabs and pizzas, which is all part of the fast-food lifestyle,' she said.

'There is easier access to fast food than 15 years ago, so much more is being eaten.

'We are also a lot less active than we have been in the past, which is a factor in changing body shapes.'

Diets do not work, she said.

'Our view is that people should maintain a healthy balanced diet throughout their life. It is about balancing food intake with energy used. Certainly yo-yo dieting is not something we would recommend at all.'

Pills are also unnecessary.

'For healthy people there is no need to take supplements. You should be able to get all the vitamins and minerals you need from a mixed diet.'

Tom Murray, head of nutrition at the FSA, said although the public knows about healthy eating, there is little change on the national menu.

'The real difficulty is achieving behavioural change,' he said. 'We need to know why it is that, despite knowing what we should be doing, for various reasons we choose not to.'

■ Written by Sean Poulter, Consumer Affairs Correspondent

© *The Daily Mail* December, 2002

# Ten steps to positive body image

*One list cannot automatically tell you how to turn negative body thoughts into positive body image, but it can help you think about new ways of looking more healthfully and happily at yourself and your body. The more you do that, the more likely you are to feel good about who you are and the body you naturally have.*

1   Appreciate all that your body can do. Every day your body carries you closer to your dreams. Celebrate all of the amazing things your body does for you – running, dancing, breathing, laughing, dreaming, etc.

2.  Keep a top-10 list of things you like about yourself – things that aren't related to how much you weigh or what you look like. Read your list often. Add to it as you become aware of more things to like about you.

3   Remind yourself that 'true beauty' is not simply skin-deep. When you feel good about yourself and who you are, you carry yourself with a sense of confidence, self-acceptance, and openness that makes you beautiful regardless of whether you physically look like a supermodel. Beauty is a state of mind, not a state of your body.

4   Look at yourself as a whole person. When you see yourself in a mirror or in your mind, choose not to focus on specific body parts. See yourself as you want others to see you – as a whole person.

5   Surround yourself with positive people. It is easier to feel good about yourself and your body when you are around others who are supportive and who recognise the importance of liking yourself just as you naturally are.

6   Shut down those voices in your head that tell you your body is not 'right' or that you are a 'bad' person. You can overpower those negative thoughts with positive ones. The next time you start to tear yourself down, build yourself back up with a few quick affirmations that work for you.

7   Wear clothes that are comfortable and that make you feel good about your body. Work with your body, not against it.

8   Become a critical viewer of social and media messages. Pay attention to images, slogans, or attitudes that make you feel bad about yourself or your body. Protest these messages: write a letter to the advertiser or talk back to the image or message.

9   Do something nice for yourself – something that lets your body know you appreciate it. Take a bubble bath, make time for a nap, find a peaceful place outside to relax.

10  Use the time and energy that you might have spent worrying about food, calories, and your weight to do something to help others. Sometimes reaching out to other people can help you feel better about yourself and can make a positive change in our world.

---

**Remind yourself that 'true beauty' is not simply skin-deep. Beauty is a state of mind, not a state of your body**

---

■ The above information is from the National Eating Disorders Association's web site which can be found at www.NationalEatingDisorders.org

*© Reprinted with permission from the National Eating Disorders Association*

Evidence from research suggests that:

– Over half of all women in Britain are either overweight or obese.

– One in three girls aged eleven are overweight.

– Among 16- to 24-year-olds, twice as many young women as young men are seriously obese. (p. 1)

– Obesity is a condition in which a person's weight gain seriously endangers their health. (p. 1)

■ Research evidence suggests that obesity has a direct link with poverty. The lower the income, the higher the tendency towards a fast-food diet with little nutritional value. (p. 2)

■ A recent survey of the diet and nutrition of young people aged 4-18 found that their diets tend to be high in saturated fats, sugar and salt. (p. 2)

■ Childhood obesity in Britain has reached epidemic levels and is likely to become even more common as children become less active. (p. 4)

■ 'Both parents and children are much less active than they were, the environment now promotes obesity in a way that it did not do before.' (p. 4)

■ Adolescents are becoming 'massively obese' at a very young age in America, a trend that is being mirrored in Britain, where more than one-fifth of the population is now clinically obese. (p. 5)

■ The 30,000 people who die each year for obesity-related reasons in Britain have had nine years cut off their lifespan and the number and reduction in lifespan are likely to increase. (p. 5)

■ An extraordinary rise in the numbers of the overweight and obese has taken place in the last 20 years. In 1980 6% of men and 8% of women were overweight. By the mid 1980s, that had doubled. Now 65.5% of men and 55.2% of women are overweight or obese in the UK, and the numbers are climbing. (p. 6)

■ Between 1993 and 2000, the numbers of young men aged 16 to 24 classified as obese – with a body mass index of more than 30 – jumped from 4.9% to 9.3%. The rise in the 25 to 34 age group in the same seven years was from 10% to 20.3%. (p. 6)

■ Evidence is now emerging to suggest that the prevalence of overweight and obesity is rising dramatically worldwide and that the problem appears to be increasing rapidly in children as well as in adults. (p. 8)

■ In 1995, there were an estimated 200 million obese adults worldwide and another 18 million under-five children classified as overweight. As of 2000, the number of obese adults has increased to over 300 million. (p. 10)

■ Obesity in the young is now seen as a soaring health crisis, with one in five of all nine-year-olds estimated to be overweight, and one in 10 obese – a rate that has doubled in the last two decades. (p. 11)

■ The incidence of obesity in England has trebled in the last 20 years. (p. 12)

■ Obesity was the cause of 18 million days of sickness absence in 1998 and 40,000 lost years of working life. (p. 12)

■ By 2010 obesity and its consequences are expected to cost the economy more than £3.6 billion a year. (p. 12)

■ Any diet on which you eat fewer calories than you need to get through the day without feeling like you're going to keel over – like an 800-calorie-per-day diet, for instance – is dangerous. (p. 13)

■ Britons were on the way to becoming the fattest people in Europe, and catching up with the United States, which has the world's heaviest population. (p. 14)

■ Anorexia is a serious condition, and not merely an obsession with weight or slimming. (p. 15)

■ Anorexia and bulimia are not new conditions. Nevertheless, they appear to be becoming more and more prevalent among young females in Western society. (p. 16)

■ Approximately 10% of people with eating disorders are men and approximately 20% of men with eating disorders identify as gay, which is double the proportion of gay men in the population. (p. 21)

■ Anorexia, bulimia and compulsive overeating can kill those who suffer from them. eating disorders have the highest rate of death out of any other psychological illness. Up to 30% of the sufferers of eating disorders (and maybe higher) will die as a result of a complication caused by the illness. (p. 23)

■ On average it takes 6 years to recover from anorexia nervosa. (p. 29)

■ While the alarm was raised this week about 75 per cent of Britons being obese by 2020, an epidemic of young women suffering from anorexia is also sweeping the land: one in 10 girls under 21 have been diagnosed with anorexia. Both trends reveal our unhealthy relationship with food. (p. 33)

■ Girls as young as seven risk developing eating disorders because they think they are too fat, a study has found. (p. 34)

■ A recent study on body image, eating disorders and the media found that many models and actresses, who are commonly cited as popular role models by young girls, have 10-15% of their body composition as fat whereas the average proportion of body fat for a healthy woman is between 22-26%. (p. 37)

■ A recent government survey reporting on the diets of British schoolchildren found that one in six girls aged 15-18 years were dieting to lose weight. (p. 37)

■ The number of women on a diet has doubled in the past 15 years. (p. 38)

■ One in five men eats no fruit at all in a week, while 15 per cent of women also fall into this category. (p. 38)

# ADDITIONAL RESOURCES

You might like to contact the following organisations for further information. Due to the increasing cost of postage, many organisations cannot respond to enquiries unless they receive a stamped, addressed envelope.

### Anorexia Bulimia Care (ABC)
PO Box 173
Letchworth
Hertfordshire
SG6 1XQ
Tel: 01462 423351
E-mail: abc@virgin.net
Web site:
www.anorexiabulimiacare.co.uk
Anorexia and Bulimia Care (ABC) has been in existence in its present form since 1989. It is a national Christian organisation run by Christians for sufferers, their families and for carers.

### British Nutrition Foundation (BNF)
High Holborn House
52-54 High Holborn
London
WC1V 6RQ
Tel: 020 7404 6504
Fax: 020 7404 6747
E-mail: postbox@nutrition.org.uk
Web site: www.nutrition.org.uk
The (BNF) is an independent charity which provides reliable information and advice on nutrition and related health matters. They produce a wide range of leaflets, briefing papers and books. Ask for their publications list.

### Eating Disorders Association (EDA)
1st Floor, Wensum House
103 Prince of Wales Road
Norwich
Norfolk
NR1 1DW
Tel: 01603 619090
Fax: 01603 664915
E-mail: info@edauk.com
Web site: www.edauk.com
Eating Disorders Association aims to be the leading charitable organisation providing comprehensive information and support for people affected by eating disorders and to influence acitvely public understanding and policy.

Telephone helplines 0845634 1414 (helpline - open 8.30am to 8.30pm Weekdays) 0845634 7650 (Youthline Callers 18 & under – open 4.00pm to 6.3 0pm Weekdays)

### European Food Information Council (EUFIC)
1 Place des Pyramides 75001
Paris
France
Tel: + 33 140 20 44 40
Fax: + 33 140 20 44 41
E-mail: eufic@eufic.org
Web site: www.eufic.org
EUFIC is a non-profit making organisation based in Paris. It has been established to provide science-based information on foods and food-related topics i.e. nutrition and health, food safety and quality and biotechnology in food for the attention of European consumers. It publishes regular newsletters, leaflets, reviews, case studies and other background information on food issues.

### National Centre for Eating Disorders
54 New Road
Esher
Surrey
KT10 9NU
Tel: 01372 469493
Fax: 01372 469550
E-mail: ncfed.globalnet.co.uk
Web site: www.eating-disorders.org.uk
The National Centre For Eating Disorders, established in 1984, is an independent organisation set up to provide solutions for all eating problems; compulsive or 'binge' eating, 'failed' or yo-yo dieting, bulimia and anorexia.

### National Eating Disorders Association
603 Stewart Street
Suite 803
Seattle
WA 98101
USA
Tel: + 1 206 382 3587
Fax: + 1 206 829 8501
E-mail:
info@NationalEatingDisorders.org
Web site:
www.nationaleatingdisorders.org
The National Eating Disorders Association (NEDA) is the largest not-for-profit organisation in the United States working to prevent eating disorders and provide treatment referrals to those suffering from anorexia, bulimia and binge eating disorder and those concerned with body image and weight issues.

### Social Issues Research Centre (SIRC)
28 St Clements
Oxford
OX4 1AB
Tel: 01865 262255
Web site: www.sirc.org
The Social Issues Research Centre was established to conduct research and promote debate on all aspects of lifestyles and social behaviour. SIRC aims to provide new insights on current social and cultural trends, and to present a balanced perspective on key social issues.

### YWCA
Clarendon House
52 Cornmarket Street
Oxford
OX1 3EJ
Tel: 01865 304200
Fax: 01865 204805
E-mail: info@ywca-gb.org.uk
Web site: www.ywca-gb.org.uk
The YWCA in England and Wales is a force for change for women who are facing discrimination and inequalities of all kinds.

# INDEX

alcohol consumption, and obesity 2
anorexia nervosa 1, 13, 15, 33
    age of onset 17
    and attitudes to food 33
    and body image 36
    and bulimia 15-16
    case study of 18-19
    and EED (extreme eating disorder) 24-5
    prevalence of 16
    preventing 26
    purging type 22
    recovery 26
    and restriction of food and calories 22
    risk of developing 20
    treatment 26, 29
anxiety, and eating disorders 20

binge-eating disorder 16
bloodletting, and EED (extreme eating disorder) 24, 25
body image 31-2
    and children 34
    and dieting 35, 38
    and eating disorders 32, 34, 36, 37
    influence of models on 36-7
    and the media 31, 34, 39
    negative 32
    positive 32
        ten steps to 39
    and self-esteem 31-2
Body Mass Index (BMI) 6, 7, 12, 14, 34
body weight
    and eating disorders 22
    and energy balance 7-8
    *see also* obesity
boys
    and body image 34
    and physical activity 2
bulimia nervosa 13, 15
    age of onset 17
    and anorexia 15-16
    and EED (extreme eating disorder) 24-5
    prevalence of 16
    preventing 26
    and purging 23
    recovery 26
    risk of developing 20
    treatment 26

cancer, and obesity 6, 7, 9
child abuse, and eating disorders 17, 20
children
    and eating disorders 34
    obesity in 4-5, 11
compulsive overeating 2, 9, 16, 17, 23
deaths
    from eating disorders 23
    obesity-related 5, 12

depression, and eating disorders 16, 20
developing countries, obesity in 10
diabetes, and obesity 1, 4, 5, 6, 7, 8, 11
diet
    British schoolchildren 37
    and obesity
        in children 4, 5
        and the food industry 6, 11, 14
        in girls and young women 2
dieting
    advice for teenagers 13-14
    and body image 32, 38
    danger signs 14
    and energy balance 7-8
    girls and young women 2, 13, 35
    and healthy eating 38
    and weight loss 13
    and women 38
discrimination, and obese people 9
diuretic pills, and eating disorders 24-5
drugs, obesity 5

eating disorders 15-30
    association with specific occupations 20, 21
    binge-eating disorder 16, 23
    and body image 32, 37
    and body weight 22
    causes of 17
    and children 34
    common misconceptions about 22-3
    compulsive overeating 2, 9, 16, 17, 23
    danger signs 14
    deaths from 23
    eating 'normally' around others 23
    health consequences of 23
    helping friends with 27
    and junk food 22
    and low calorie intake 22
    and mealtimes 28-9
    and men 16, 20, 21, 30
    overcoming 17
    and physical or sexual abuse 17, 20
    prevention 26, 30
    questions of carers and families about 28-9
    recovery from 26, 29
    risks of developing 20
    teenagers and dieting 13
    types of people suffering from 22
    and vitamin supplements 23
    women and extreme eating disorders 24-5
    *see also* anorexia nervosa; bulimia nervosa; obesity
EEDs (extreme eating disorders) 24-5
energy balance, and weight loss 7-8
ethnic minorities, obesity in young women 1, 2
exercise
    compulsive 23

and obesity, in girls and young women 1, 2, 2-3
    physical activity referral schemes 14

fast foods
    and dieting 38
    and obesity 6, 33-4
fat in the diet, and obesity, in girls and young women 2
food, British attitudes to 33-4
food industry
    and obesity 6
      advertising junk food 11, 14

gay men, and eating disorders 21
girls and young women
    and body image 34
    and dieting 2, 13, 35
    and eating disorders 15-19, 20, 22-30, 35
    and obesity 1-3, 6
GPs (general practitioners), and eating disorders 21, 28

health
    and obesity 1, 8-9, 10, 12, 14, 37
      in children 4, 5, 11
healthy eating, and dieting 38
heart disease
    and eating disorders 37
    and obesity 6, 7, 8-9, 37
      in children 4, 5
      in women 1
high blood pressure, and obesity in women 1

junk food 38
    advertising, and children 11, 14, 34
    and eating disorders 22

lifestyle
    and obesity 6
      in children 4, 11
      in girls and young women 2
    promoting healthy lifestyles 9
low self-esteem
    and eating disorders 17, 23
    and obesity
      in children 4
      in girls and young women 3

media
    and body image 31, 34, 39
      and eating disorders 37
    and dieting 35
men
    and body image 31
    and eating disorders 16, 20, 21, 30
    and healthy eating 38
    and obesity
      fat distribution 7
      rates of 8, 10, 12
    obesity in young men 6
mothers
    and children's diets 4
    eating habits 2
NHS (National Health Service)
    and obesity 12
      in children 11

obesity 1-14
    and attitudes to food 33-4
    and Body Mass Index (BMI) 6, 7, 12, 14, 34
    in children 4-5, 11
    controlling the global epidemic 10
    defining 7, 12
    drugs 5
    economic cost of 9, 12
    and fat distribution 7
    in girls and young women 1-3, 6
      psycho-social effects of 3
      rise in 1-2
    health consequences of 1, 8-9, 10, 12, 14, 37
      and children 4, 5, 11
    human cost of 12
    and overweight 7-9
    prevalence of 5, 6, 8, 12, 14
    psychological aspects of 9
    tackling obesity in England 12
    in young men 6

osteoarthritis, and obesity 1, 9

parents, and obesity in children 5, 11
personality, and EED (extreme eating disorder) 25
physical activity see exercise
poverty, and obesity 1, 2

schools
    children walking to school 2
    participation in school sports 2-3
self-esteem
    and body image 31-2
    and eating disorders 29
    see also low self-esteem
self-harm, and EED (extreme eating disorder) 25
smoking, and obesity 2
social class, and obesity 1-2
social exclusion, and obesity 1
sport, participation in school sports 2-3
sports centres and clubs, and young women 3

therapy, for eating disorders 29

vegetarians, and dieting 14
vitamin supplements
    and eating disorders 23
    and healthy eating 38

waist measurement, and obesity 7
walking, children walking to school 2
women
    and body image 31
    and dieting 38
    and extreme eating disorders 24-5
    and healthy eating 38
    and obesity
      and cancer 9
      and diabetes 1, 8
      and fat distribution 7
      rates of 8, 10, 12
      super-obese women 6
    see also girls and young women

# ACKNOWLEDGEMENTS

The publisher is grateful for permission to reproduce the following material.

While every care has been taken to trace and acknowledge copyright, the publisher tenders its apology for any accidental infringement or where copyright has proved untraceable. The publisher would be pleased to come to a suitable arrangement in any such case with the rightful owner.

### Chapter One: Obesity

*Obesity*, © YWCA, *Childhood obesity at 'epidemic' levels*, © Guardian Newspapers Limited 2003, *Overweight or obese young adults*, © Crown copyright is reproduced with the permission of Her Majesty's Stationery Office, *Parents to 'outlive obese youngsters'*, © Telegraph Group Limited, London 2003, *Food industry blamed for surge in obesity*, © Guardian Newspapers Limited 2003, *Obesity*, © 2003 EUFIC, *Risk of associated diseases of obesity*, © Crown copyright is reproduced with the permission of Her Majesty's Stationery Office, *Obesity and overweight*, © World Health Organization (WHO), *Global prevalence of obesity in adults*, © International Obesity Task Force, *NHS wakes up to child obesity crisis*, © Guardian Newspapers Limited 2003, *Tackling obesity in England*, © Crown copyright is reproduced with the permission of Her Majesty's Stationery Office, *Obesity factfile*, © Crown copyright is reproduced with the permission of Her Majesty's Stationery Office, *The deal with diets*, © KidsHealth.org, *20 pc of Britons will be clinically obese by 2017*, © Telegraph Group Limited, London 2003.

### Chapter Two: Eating Disorders

*About eating disorders . . .*, © 2003 Anorexia Bulimia Care, *Causes of eating disorders*, © 2003 Anorexia Bulimia Care, *Fighting Anna*, © Eating Disorders Association (EDA), *Risks*, © ANRED Anorexia Nervosa and Related Eating Disorders, Inc., *Men get eating disorders too*, © Eating Disorders Association (EDA), *Common misconceptions*, © Something Fishy Music & Publishing. All rights reserved, *Women who go to extremes to lose weight*, © The Scotsman, November 2002, *Thin is not the answer*, © 2001-2003 PPFA. All rights reserved, *I think my friend may have an eating disorder*, © KidsHealth.org, *Carers' questions*, © King's College London, *Eating disorders can be prevented!*, © 2003 National Eating Disorders Association.

### Chapter Three: Body Image

*Body image*, © 2003 National Centre for Eating Disorders, *Body image*, © 2003 National Eating Disorders Association, *The fat of the land*, © Guardian Newspapers Limited 2003, *Body mass*, © Crown copyright is reproduced with the permission of Her Majesty's Stationery Office, *Young girls who think they are too fat to be perfect*, © The Daily Mail, June 2003, *Don't put your daughter on a diet*, © Social Issues Research Centre, *You are not a model, you are a real person!*, © 1999-2003 Pupiline Limited, *Body image and eating disorders*, © British Nutrition Foundation (BNF), *Image obsession*, © The Daily Mail, December 2002, *Ten steps to positive image*, © 2003 National Eating Disorders Association.

### Photographs and illustrations:

Pages 1, 22, 30, 38: Pumpkin House; pages 5, 15, 23, 26, 29, 31, 39: Simon Kneebone; pages 6, 18, 28, 36: Bev Aisbett.

Craig Donnellan
Cambridge
September, 2003